D1323272

BIAS IMPACTS:

How Culture and Diversity Affect the Leadership Journey

Kanthi Ford and **Patrick Ricketts**

authorHOUSE·

AuthorHouse™ UK
1663 Liberty Drive
Bloomington, IN 47403 USA
www.authorhouse.co.uk
Phone: UK TFN: 0800 0148641 (Toll Free inside the UK)
UK Local: (02) 0369 56322 (+44 20 3695 6322 from outside the UK)

© 2023 Kanthi Ford and Patrick Ricketts. All rights reserved.

No part of this book may be reproduced, stored in a retrieval system, or transmitted by any means without the written permission of the author.

Published by AuthorHouse 06/02/2023

ISBN: 979-8-8230-8166-5 (sc)
ISBN: 979-8-8230-8167-2 (hc)
ISBN: 979-8-8230-8168-9 (e)

Print information available on the last page.

Any people depicted in stock imagery provided by Getty Images are models, and such images are being used for illustrative purposes only. Certain stock imagery © Getty Images.

This book is printed on acid-free paper.

Because of the dynamic nature of the Internet, any web addresses or links contained in this book may have changed since publication and may no longer be valid. The views expressed in this work are solely those of the author and do not necessarily reflect the views of the publisher, and the publisher hereby disclaims any responsibility for them.

Contents

About the Book and the Authors

In 2020 and 2021, the worldwide COVID-19 pandemic combined with globalisation and information technology disruption has given rise to the most radical reinvention of the working environment since the Industrial Revolution. The time of the hierarchical organisation that was male dominated, with autocratic leadership styles, is well and truly moving on.

The concepts underpinning diversity, equity, and inclusion are used extensively in business circles. The impacts of some these unconscious biases are rather more intangible. So, this book was written by our two authors, Kanthi Ford and Patrick Ricketts, to open a window and provide some insights into some workplace realities.

Kanthi and Patrick are both company directors. They met at an online directors' forum during the pandemic. They were musing about the fact that most people at the session were typical of workplaces they had encountered – all white and predominantly male. Then it occurred to them that by sharing their lived experiences, they might provide some understanding of the challenges that people like them encounter through unconscious bias. Kanthi is a leadership and business development coach, so it was decided to frame their personal experiences in becoming company directors, placing these stories within the context of developing leaders who are more aware and so able to transform their organisations to be truly diverse, equitable, and inclusive.

We would recommend this easy read to anyone who is curious about the impact of their decisions on the people around them. The book draws heavily on the individual experiences of the authors as they journey through their careers. Kanthi Ford has been a company director for twenty years. She has worked in television, advertising, and organisational restructuring.

More recently, she has been working as a strategic consultant and business executive coach advising companies on cultural transformation.

Patrick Ricketts started his career as an apprentice toolmaker qualifying as a bench fitter designing and making press tools. He moved on to production management in the manufacturing sector before moving to the service sector then subsequently to the construction sector. Today, he is an accomplished director who has spent twenty-five years in commercial and operational leadership roles restructuring businesses for sustainable growth in the UK and working across Ireland and Northern Europe.

How to Get the Most Value

In this roller coaster of global business change, nobody can manage the way they did before the 2020 coronavirus pandemic and the emergence of the Black Lives Matter movement. Now is the time to embrace new ways of leading, new ways to encourage diversity, equity, and inclusion, while encouraging innovation, in the workforce, new ways to help people thrive in an endlessly changing environment, new ways to create a high-performing business. The disintegration of traditional hierarchies has now become inevitable. Our aim is to help you in discovering new routes to future success.

The following chapters will lead you through many simple, common-sense concepts that are fundamental to leading in a diverse, equitable, and inclusive workplace. They are equally critical for you on a personal basis whether at work or at home. Sprinkled throughout are questions which may help you consider your situation in a different light and suggested actions which may help you in shifting your behaviours or understanding the perspectives of those whom you lead.

This book will enable you to understand more about yourself, your style, and how to deal with and influence other people. You can learn how to be more inclusive and less biased. You can learn how to lead through change and get more results. We suggest you read the following materials in short segments and take the time to reflect in between. Use it as a tool to expand your leadership knowledge. Learn ways to apply some diversity, equity, and inclusion concepts to your personal life. Maybe share it with your team and use it as a tool for discussion. Either way, this book will be an investment in your personal growth and development. The dividends will be considerable.

Culture and Diversity: How Bias Affects the Journey to the Top

Preface

It was a sunny morning as the last vestiges of winter were being replaced by spring sunshine, with all its implicit hopefulness, a Tuesday in March, the kind of day that makes people hopeful for new beginnings. I was going to a meeting with the head of HR to discuss my contract renewal. I had been working with this television company for six months. I needed to understand what the future path would be.

The meeting had unwound – the stuttering start, cursory greetings, the necessary preamble, my request for a future route map. Then came the two startling comments that were to hold a mirror up to my life and seed my destiny:

"We hired you to look good for diversity."

"The best way to get to the top in this business is to sleep your way there. I can suggest one or two people that may be able to help."

The memory of that encounter has stayed with me throughout my career. When I entered that office, I was in my first career job since I had finished my university degree – but there was scant attention paid to political correctness, let alone individual respect. Human resources were perceived as a function of administration and logistics rather than the science of talent management and people protocol. Yet imagine my shock at the statements!

My background, and the way that I was wired, meant that I was determined to achieve success without taking his advice. It left me feeling vulnerable and quite traumatised. Yet I dismissed him as misguided and was determined to prove him wrong. Success did arrive eventually.

Years later, I was running a leadership workshop with young engineers at a conference focussed on equality and diversity in the energy sector. When I shared this story, the audible gasp in the room demonstrated just how much the business world has moved on since that fateful meeting at the end of seventies.

Each day's news comes to us rife with such reports revealing lack of respect, implicit and explicit racism, the disintegration of the older orders, an onslaught of view and counterview, well-meaning intention running amok. But the news simply reflects to us, on a larger scale, a creeping sense of massive change. Meanwhile, businesses and governments call out for political correctness, increased unconscious-bias trainings, and diversity and inclusion quotas.

This book talks of ethnic diversity and to a lesser extent gender differences in the workplace. It is a compilation of lived experiences to provide insights or make sense of the senseless. It shares discussions between Ella NilaKanthi Ford (a part-Asian woman) and Patrick Ricketts (UK-second-generation Jamaican). We met as directors of different organisations, and during many a conversation, we came to believe that our personal experiences might shine a light for today's decision-makers. During the process of writing this book, we also travelled personal journeys of discovery and insight.

Why Now?

The last decade has seen a stream of scientific studies on emotion and bias. Studies of the brain have, for the first time, made visible how we think, feel, and respond. This type of data enables us to understand how the deep-seated wiring of the brain channels us, for better or worse.

This information is also coupled with extensive research into the management of organisational culture, combined with an understanding of national cultures. It will help to inform organisational decision-makers as they move forward.

Our Journeys

In this book, we serve as guides, two very different people, with inside knowledge acquired on our journeys, through two unconnected careers from school to board. It is our lived learnings. We would like to believe it will provide our personal insights into ethnic diversity and male/female gender issues. This will help you to lead organisations with greater awareness of diversity, equity, and inclusion. It will also provide you with a way to put yourself in someone else's shoes.

The journey's end is to understand what it means to be a person from an ethnic minority or a woman in business, or both, and how to encourage genuine equality at the board level. Our journey in seven chapters begins with a description of our employment experiences throughout our careers and opens a window on the unconscious barriers to career progression. We discuss unconscious bias and the way the brain functions when experiencing moments of the unknown or of difference. We reveal how much our instinctive responses can undermine best intentions. Most importantly, we suggest simple steps for shaping future interactions.

We take you through several discussions that build on this. We hope it will provide a clearer understanding of the challenges faced by ethnic minorities and women in the workplace whilst embracing the differences they can bring in leadership roles. It also provides you with some tips as to how you can nurture this talent and grow personally.

Chapter 1, 'People (Who Are) Like Them', examines the issues created by unconscious bias and describes some of the pitfalls experienced in companies recruiting people of a similar appearance and gender. It asks you what you would do differently and reviews some aspects that may be a barrier to be an inclusive board member. We talk about the changing business environment and the shifting role of leaders. We provide various doors and windows through which you can look to re-evaluate yourself as a leader rather than a boss.

Chapter 2 helps you explore your role as an empathic leader. It suggests things that you can do to engage more effectively with your peers, team members, and colleagues. It introduces the concept of the shadow you cast as a leader and how you can leverage it for maximum effect.

Chapter 3 debates the question 'Does Activism Reinforce Bias?' In this chapter, we discuss company cultures and managing uncertainty as well as our evolving views on activism, together with our experiences of tokenism in the context of our careers. Whilst we would like to explore company culture and societal influences, we believe that is a subject for others. Hopefully, by examining some aspects of corporate culture, we can start to understand the bigger societal picture, but, first, let's explore activism. In chapter 4, 'Streets or Establishment?' we explore the need for vision, both for individual development as well as for changes in business and in society. We also highlight our personal experiences of systemic racism in the community and in education in the hope that evidence like this may identify the barriers facing some young people and point to the resources that can be used to overcome these difficulties.

Chapter 5, 'Is Speaking Up Worth Losing Your Job For?' considers the appropriateness of standing up for personal values. When do you start to say, 'No, this is not acceptable behaviour,' and start standing up for what is right? When do you start to own the situation and take accountability for some of the outcomes? What are some of the changes needed in leadership teams and organisational cultures that will create a springboard for the shifts in behaviour necessary to give everyone the confidence to speak up and build accountability?

Relationships are the touchstone for chapter 6. We explore some basic principles of personal style and personality. We then provide some tools to consider how you might interact with all the diversity of people in your life. Chapter 7 encapsulates the original purpose of this book – to change people's views on diversity, equity, and inclusion. It brings the reader up to date with recent experiences described. It also touches on some key behaviours necessary for you to develop psychologically safe environments for others. It concludes with a summary of the book. Most important, it provocatively challenges the reader to take action to do things differently and become an authentic leader who embraces diversity, equity, and inclusion.

CHAPTER 1

People (Who Are) like Them

This chapter provides the personal points of view of our authors as recipients of personal bias and how we were affected. It then goes on to explore unconscious bias and what it really means for a leader today. We ask what you would do differently and review some aspects that may be barriers to being an inclusive board member. We talk about the changing business environment and the shifting role of leaders. We provide various doors and windows through which you can look to re-evaluate yourself as a leader rather than a boss.

How the New Order Affects Leadership

Today there is increasing focus on businesses which are diverse, equitable, and inclusive (D, E, and I) in culture. Companies are encouraged to have policies which will underpin this shift in organisational culture so that everyone is included in an equitable fashion and diversity is embraced not avoided. This is the new order in brief.

As a reader, you may be aware of diversity, equity, and inclusion and its importance, but how much are you really supporting it? People today are wired to challenge more and to focus on their quality of life. Meantime, companies are hiring people to work virtually without acknowledging the social context of the countries their employees operate from. It is little wonder that effective business leadership has become far more complex.

Most executives will agree that the older style business clichés will not be appropriate for, or even fit into, today's business world. This is true when dealing with customers, colleagues, or peers. People have different expectations. Social culture has shifted. The old management styles are struggling to keep up. For earlier generations, organisations had more hierarchical us-and-them structures. They were more likely to accept authority and consequent discrimination without question.

The examples from our authors below are from a generation ago. Unfortunately, some of these behaviours persist. Kanthi explains a recent example: 'This last fortnight I have been visiting the regional offices of an old-style company at locations all across the UK. I was running focus groups to gain an understanding how the workforce approached their work. The company nominated various team members for representative perspectives. In the whole two weeks, I did not have the opportunity to interview any women or people from ethnic-minority backgrounds. It was meeting after meeting with white men over forty years old or under thirty. The management team all looked very similar. The only women I saw were staff who had been tasked with organising refreshments for the sessions. Whilst the team members had no issues dealing with me asking some challenging questions, it was like I had gone back in time.

'In contrast, I also work with a company which is multinational and where there are as many women as men in the management team. Here hierarchy is challenged and people work together in meetings supportively.'

Patrick observes, 'The management team spent more time with people who looked like them, not me. In the end, it made me more determined to prove what I could do. After that, I also became more of a risk-taker when making career moves.'

Kanthi adds, 'I was told I ticked both gender and ethnicity boxes when I joined – told not once but multiple times – by so many of my new colleagues. How do you think that made me feel? When I got over feeling like my appointment was all about being a token senior woman or a token ethnic minority, I still felt lucky to have the opportunity. It made me determined to prove that I could be 'the best' – whatever that meant for me at the time.'

Patrick continues, 'I joined a company with a management title (in name only) as the only non-white, office-based person. I did what was required of me well. Within six months, a white graduate, who had never worked in his life, joined as a senior manager with all the usual benefits.

'I was not invited to interview for the promotion. Instead, the business owner introduced me to the new manager. He said, "I want you to train him." Why would I want to do that? The business owner recognised that I had ability to do things well. However, he was not willing to consider progression for me. I never hung around to find out why and eventually moved on.'

Kanthi continues, 'My pet hates? People telling me I speak good English. Worse still? When asked where I come from, and I answer, "England," the next question being, "Yes but where are you really from?" I hear it most weeks, not just in the UK, even in 2021.'

Kanthi adds, 'A few weeks ago, I was at a dinner where comedian Lenny Henry was an after-dinner speaker. In addition to promoting the work of Comic Relief, a charity set up to raise funds to create a just world free from poverty, he was humorously sharing anecdotes from his childhood and being a Jamaican child growing up in northern Britain, probably at the same time as Patrick. During and after the presentation, my dinner companions were heckling him, claiming that they were already doing diversity. The after-dinner conversation was started by the sentiment that they wished the comedian would stick to being funny and not challenge industry's approach to diversity. I looked round the room, almost a thousand people, mainly white men in dinner suits, were evident.

Understanding Unconscious Bias

Unconscious bias is what it says on the tin. It is bias that individuals are completely unaware of. People form social stereotypes in their own conscious awareness. This is typically based on the beliefs and values they have developed since birth. This bias is enhanced by the brain's tendency to wish to categorise everything.

Everyone holds these unconscious beliefs about various social and identity groups. These can range from favouring one gender over another (gender bias), ageism, name bias, beauty bias, halo effect, horns effect, confirmation bias, conformity bias.

For example, racial bias occurs when someone makes a statement like, "When I look at you, I don't see colour." These sorts of comments remove the acknowledgment of a person's skin colour and invalidate their racial, ethnic, and cultural identity, which, in turn, can be an important part of their lived experience.

As insights into the impact of unconscious bias, Patrick and Kanthi's examples testify to the personal and societal legacies perpetuated by people working in companies the world over. In an era where transactional, economic relationships were the managerial norm (you work – you get paid), work was a social system. People wanted to engage with their peers while paying lip service to 'the boss'.

Today the workplace is very different. As society changes, employees change. It is accepted that people are more knowledgeable, or at least internet savvy. They will ask more questions and seek to challenge the status quo. Companies ask for commitment and engagement while continuing to ignore the social context of the cultures of their people as well as the corporate culture they are expected to work in. Leading a business effectively whilst striving for a culture of diversity, equity, and inclusion has become a far more complex activity.

Diversity, Equity, and Inclusion and the Brain

The brain has evolved over time. Studies have made it clear that the human brain is a social structure. Its physiological and neurological reactions are honed through social human interaction. This presents challenges for managers who have been used to basing business relationships on transactional criteria. People denied the appropriate social context can experience real feelings of rejection, pain, and discomfort. So, the interaction between a manager and their team must make suitable allowances to accommodate interaction.

Leaders who understand the social dynamic required by the human brain can effectively build employee engagement and commitment. They can foster a diverse, inclusive, and productive culture. The impact on the social brain of the risk/reward response is also an interesting consideration in this arena. The limbic system is a primitive part of the brain common

4

to animals. It becomes aroused when it perceives a threat. Neurons are activated and hormones released as the brain tries to determine whether the *threat* represents reward or danger. This fight-or-flight response can be unconscious and is activated rapidly and emotionally. So if one's brain sees a threat to survival, whether it is feeling hunger, being ostracized, or being placed in an unfamiliar environment, even having to work with people who are unlike oneself, the brain will activate similar neural responses.

This manifests itself in organisations through tribal behaviours – different tribes with contrasting behaviours – with consequent in-groups and out-groups. In social psychology, an in-group are people who identify with each other based on a variety of factors including gender, race, religion, or geography. These group identifications can promote a sense of identity and belonging identities which helps us define ourselves and enables others to define us. They can also raise self-esteem and sense of status. This leads to comparisons between *people like us* and people who are different. You can observe this in *us*-and-*them* thinking and behaviours worldwide.

Every human carries implicit bias with them every day. Biases are socially learned stereotypes so embedded in our belief systems that everything we see and hear around us is filtered to reinforce them. Often based on deep-seated, neural wiring, this has in many instances become automatic.

Biases impact everything around us, from personal and professional relationships to simple or complex decisions, and even scientific research. They can also impact every aspect of workplace culture, through hiring practices, promotions, pay structure, and productivity, not to mention the overall wellbeing of employees.

Unconsciously, we tend to build mental barriers where none exist. We trip over mental blocks that exclude us from the bigger picture. Individuals, divisions, and business units tend to create self-imposed, imaginary limitations to thinking. Then, in times of uncertainty, they revert to their comfort zones and old behaviour patterns or self-limiting beliefs They think, *I can only trust people like me*. The current environment of fundamental global reinvention amidst uncertainty makes it essential to shift the old-world order.

Leadership to Look at Things Differently

Everyone needs to understand the differences required in leadership today. From focussing on the transactional, process-driven aspects of the organisation, leaders now need to focus on their relationships and influencing skills. We should all consciously improve our skills in leading equal, diverse, and inclusive cultures.

Studies are now being carried out that explore the connection between diversity, equity, and inclusion and high-performing businesses. For instance, an article by FDM Group argues the case for gender diversity in particular. It concludes, 'Companies in the top quartile for racial and ethnic diversity are 35% more likely, and those for gender diversity are 15% more likely, to perform above the national average financially.' Other studies examining the links between diversity and firm performance, such as that by Cornell University, explore the positive correlation between diverse leadership and financial benefit for companies. Their conclusions show a positive relationship between leader diversity and revenues. Finally in the *Harvard Business Review* 2018 article 'The Other Diversity Dividend', the authors explore the notion that varied teams do not just make better decisions – they also make better investments.

To achieve diverse leadership, it might be necessary to look at the world and its people differently. For instance, try setting up a reverse mentoring scheme with diverse ranges of people or set up some specialist community groups to embrace different ethnicities and cultural interests. This will enable an innovative organisation with motivated people focussing on delivering results. In turn, greater positive interactions will lead to increased productivity and enhanced business performance.

When Does Bias Become Stereotype?

We all struggle with implicit and explicit biases developed over time. They can become quite pervasive. However, by addressing our own personal privileges and moving beyond superficial awareness of biases, we can begin to undo their negative impacts in blinding us to opportunities and stifling innovation. The question is, who goes first, the person affected or the leader of the organisation? Who takes the risk?

The global COVID-19 pandemic and economic uncertainties have exacerbated this situation. Unfortunately, society still leans towards stereotypical gender roles and unconscious bias. More women than men on a global basis have been trying to balance business and political activities as well as home-schooling and domestic tasks. This is when gender bias overtakes stereotype.

Kanthi provides an example: 'I have coaching clients in Africa and Asia as well as Europe and the United States. They were all reporting to me that since the start of the COVID-19 pandemic and various lockdowns, the female members of staff are struggling to manage households and their usual workloads. Somehow, the lion's share of home-schooling and domestic activities seems to have devolved to the women in the households. There is some speculation that once society evolves to its new normal, the role of women in the workplace may have been set back by decades.'

In addition to the COVID-19 pandemic in 2020, the death of George Floyd precipitated the vociferous protests of the Black Lives Matter (BLM) movement. Interestingly, the global BLM protestors seemed to be of all cultures and ethnicities. These events certainly gave impetus for a wider debate on cultural diversity issues. It is positive to now hear businesses including diversity, equity, and inclusion as a key part of their corporate agendas – a long overdue step forward. Real action will take longer.

Moving into leadership roles where relationships, influencing others, and looking at the bigger picture are important, we run into challenges. Generally, in the traditional business world, this social brain is underdeveloped. Yet the new world order needs big-picture thinking. Encouraging others' points of view through diversity, equity, and inclusion will lead to more innovation and more awareness of opportunities. Other peoples' perspectives may bring several things that are ultimately critical to the success of an initiative. We can never see the whole picture. Everything we see is limited by our personal experiences, our beliefs, and our assumptions. So, by bringing a variety of perspectives into the equation you will be able to see the world differently, make more informed decisions and embrace hitherto unconsidered alternatives. It is important to be curious, listen with empathy and ask open questions of your peers and team members.

If you want to go fast, go alone. If you want to go far, go together.
– African proverb

As humans, seeing just part of the picture is the norm. Issues can arise when we believe we do see the whole picture. Drawing conclusions on that premise can lead to significant gaps in decision-making. Unfortunately, there is also limited correlation between organisational vision, values, and a company's accepted behaviours. So, talking about diversity, equity, and inclusion at the board level does not tend to convert into people embracing these principles.

Don't forget the work which has been done on the human brain. Remember the way we are wired, the social brain and the amygdala. The amygdala is constantly scanning its environment for signs of trouble. This makes the amygdala super powerful. Imagine a sensor that is, at its essence, primitive. *Is this something unknown? Is this something I should be frightened of?* the amygdala thinks. If the amygdala subconsciously elicits a yes, the human response is instantaneous. It sends urgent messages to the body, triggers fight-or-flight hormones and so on. We believe that the amygdala's ability to hijack the brain explains a great deal of irrational behaviours when it comes to bias and the diversity, equity, and inclusion agenda.

This imprecision of the emotional brain can derive from childhood memories. Blueprints are stored in an imprecise way because babies have no words to describe their experiences. So these emotional memories are triggered subconsciously and without reason when we become adults.

Unconscious bias is just one of many cognitive biases. While interpreting new information to support existing beliefs (confirmation bias), other cognitive biases can materialise as we progress through our careers. We can be aware of them. We can't remove them.

It is important to recognise that there is more to what we see individually. Our survival depends on that insight. Yet so many company systems and processes continue the bias. Recruitment and promotions tend to be swayed by bias, which we will cover later in this chapter. Also, you will still get stock answers when executives are challenged about what they are doing to evidence diversity, equity, and inclusion activities as part of normal everyday business that addresses ethnicity. Executives are more comfortable talking about and demonstrating activities around gender and disability than about race.

Let's see some of these issues. Patrick takes up the story:

'It was a long-standing family-run company of circa 150 employees based in the centre of Birmingham. Set out on two floors, the company manufactured screws and fasteners for the international market.

'Most employees operated presses producing screws, bolts, and any other items that could be made from drawn metal wire, fulfilling orders that the sales team had secured. Inspection was carried out on the second floor by low-skilled employees, all females, while finished products were warehoused and despatched from the back of the factory.

'Additionally, there were maintenance engineers who ensured that all the presses and other factory equipment were in good working order and *a tool room* with eighteen staff plus a foreman and production manager who led the tool room and the press department. The other employees in the tool room were either turners, surface grinders, or heat-treatment or spark-erosion workers.

'Six bench fitters, one of whom was a Sikh, designed and made the tooling for the presses. The office was filled with managers, administration staff, draughtsmen, and secretaries. There was one black man and one black woman.

'The company had an apprenticeship scheme for its maintenance engineers and tool room. I was one of two people recruited for the tool room, and three others joined the maintenance engineering department – two of Afro-Caribbean and one of Irish heritage.

'The five of us all went off to college together. Two were on craft engineering and three were on technical-engineering courses for our one-year, off-the-job training. I was on the craft-engineering course.

'After our first year of this three-year apprenticeship, we arrived back at the workplace and reacquainted ourselves with the mentors/trainers we had been assigned a year earlier. Before long, the other craft engineer was assigned to the office, working with the draughtsmen producing drawings from which the tool room staff would manufacture components for the press room. I was not asked and was not even aware whether I was considered for the role.

'When I asked the foreman why I was not given the same opportunity, the explanation was "he was more suited than you". It was still early in my working life, so my immediate thought was not that the person getting the role was white but that he was not particularly good on the "tools". The thoughts about discrimination came later.

'My training continued, machine by machine, and I liked the variety of that. By the end of my second year, I was being given finished sample components to design and required to make tooling to produce hundreds of thousands of components within tight deadlines. I had lots of success as well as some not so successful outcomes; however, on balance, the results were positive. As I was approaching the middle of my final year, there was talk of assigning me to one machine. This was not what I wanted or what I believed I was capable of.

'I wanted recognition for being able to do more technical things and a multitude of processes as well. As I became more confident, I started to challenge the trainers and the management team, requesting that I be allowed to perform more interesting tasks to develop my skills and experience.

'It took four years of struggle to get recognition for my ability to do the job expertly and, at times, even better than my counterparts. Throughout this time, there were neither reviews of note nor encouragement. There was quite a lot of behind-the-scenes, what would be called harassment these days. One operator did step in if he felt I was being unfairly treated by other colleagues. No manager ever got involved. This operator saw beyond colour and championed me and, in doing so, risked long-standing friendships he had built over years. I realised then that you need champions in your corner on this journey.'

Effective leaders are excellent at developing relationships and encouraging others. How would you manage this scenario as a leader or a manager? Leaders set the vision, motivate, and inspire. Managers do what it says in the title. They manage. Of course, managers can also be leaders. Leaders are self-aware and constantly seeking to learn more about themselves and others as well as the world at large. They are navigating their business and all its people through an ever-changing world and a competitive marketplace.

- Think of a time when you would have done things differently?
- Why would you have liked to do that, and what would you have done?

As a leader, your ability to motivate people and lead change is essential. The traditional, transactional functions of management – meeting targets, planning, directing, organising, delegating – have been superseded. Today, customers know a thing or two, and so do employees. So building relationships and developing as a leader instead of being a manager is essential. Shifting from being the boss to being a coach, or empowering people rather than controlling them, starts with understanding yourself and maybe some of the unconscious behaviours you have or have observed in others. That starts with understanding your beliefs and some of the possible biases you hold. Awareness of bias can start so early.

Kanthi substantiates this:

'I was born in the UK into a reasonably wealthy family in suburban Surrey. I sensed I was different at nursery because of the way some of the parents and teachers treated me. Fortunately, I believed it was because I was "special". However, at the age of four, for multiple reasons, including the belief that my father (who was Sri Lankan) was experiencing prejudice in securing employment after his university course, we moved to Ceylon, as it was called then.

'I spent my schooldays at Ladies College, Sri Lanka. In Ceylon, I was fair skinned. In England, I was dark skinned I realised early that humans can be fickle. The unconscious bias in humans is inconsistent.

'More recently, when my sister took her children to school, a teacher asked her when the children's mother would be bringing them to school! The teacher had assumed that she was the nanny. My sister was so affronted that she called me when she got home and asked if I had ever experienced a similar question.

'I just laughed and said, "Often. First with my children and then with my grandchildren." Our children are fair skinned. We are brown.'

Nonetheless, if schoolteachers are displaying such thinking, then it is inevitable that the children they are working with will absorb similar views. Bias and stereotype are all around us.

Kanthi shares another anecdote:

'Just last week as I was out walking, I happened to pass someone who lives in my street. It was a beautiful spring day. The sun was shining, and the leaves on the trees were starting to turn green. There was a gang of builders with XYZ Landscape emblazoned on their jackets, carrying out work in the grounds of a recently built apartment building. It was a hive of activity. However, I was concerned that neither of the two men cutting flags with electric grinders were wearing ear defenders or gloves.

'This neighbour must have been in his early sixties and recently retired from a successful career in business. In passing, I happened to mention to him that I was concerned about the men's future hearing loss.

'His immediate reaction was, "Oh these people hire so many foreign contractors these days," as if foreign contractors would be oblivious to safety requirements.

'I did suggest that this may have been a sweeping statement, especially as I had heard several of the men calling to each other in broad English accents. His assumption proved a stereotype that could not be substantiated.'

Stereotype and unconscious bias affect every aspect of the business world. Not only do we rarely have the complete picture, but we also often assume we are correct when we are not. The biggest hurdle to overcome is working with those people who strongly feel that they are correct. They will find it the most difficult to consider other possibilities.

Kanthi continues:

'I was working with an oil-and-gas company. Inevitably, I was based in Texas, USA, and was staying in a five-star hotel at the time. Frequently, the (mainly) male guests would address me in Spanish, asking me about linen or domestic help or catering facilities. When I amusedly shared this with an American colleague, his answer was, "Most of the hotels are staffed with Hispanics, so they would assume that's your role too."

'Several times I have been delighted to be invited as a keynote speaker at large leadership events. The first time I became aware of the stereotypical perception of me as a woman in a male-dominated organisation was more than twenty years ago. This situation has happened multiple times since, in different geographies and business sectors. However, that first occasion was a surprise.

'There was an exciting weekend of activities planned. A range of interactive sessions, video door-stepping, world-renowned speakers and receptions were all in the mix. The hotel, located near a major airport for easy access, was sumptuous. The whole hotel seemed to be buzzing with event organisers, television and stage crews, and excited men arriving, bumping into familiar colleagues, and chatting.

'I happened to be in reception talking to the event organisers about the anticipated start time for a rehearsal planned that evening. The lobby was full of people. Just then two executives arrived at the desk. As I was due to be with them on a panel the next day, I stepped forward to introduce myself.

'I was in smart business clothes, a suit and blouse. The first man in the group asked where the conference was taking place. I told him the name of the suite and then held my hand out to introduce myself.

Ignoring my hand, he said, "Can I have the check-in details?"

I laughed and turned to one of the organisers who stepped in with a welcome pack. He just walked off towards the double doors. One rude person? Unfortunately, not. Two more people behind him also asked me for their registration details. So, I gave up my quest and left for my room, smiling to myself, and thinking they would be in for a shock next day.

'So, an isolated example from twenty years ago? Regrettably not. Just recently, I was co-facilitating a workshop with a team from a major UK multinational. The group represented a cross section of the thirty-thousand-plus workforce from directors through to front line engineers. My co-facilitator was male. We presented a set of slides based on a report I had written. He talked of the theory; I shared the findings.

'Unsurprisingly, given the topic, there were lots of questions. Extremely surprising was that every single person with a question, even the women, asked my colleague. Each time, he answered on the theory and handed it over to me for the detail saying, "Kanthi has more knowledge on this." Each time, they addressed him. Now, we can speculate on these behaviours, and to be honest, as a younger woman I would have thought it reflected my competence. However, it was far more likely that in a hierarchical, male-dominated business, attendees were behaving like the generations before them.'

Diversity, equity, and inclusion are fundamental to business growth and should not be ignored. Increasingly, companies are hiring diversity, equity, and inclusion heads, but they need budget and a genuine desire to succeed. I have heard more than one human resources leader recently complain that diversity and inclusion make a louder noise than other areas in the organisation saying 'We don't want people outside waving placards because they think we are not being inclusive enough.' This is not motivating companies to embrace diversity, equity, and inclusion; this is merely tokenism to protect reputation.

What Do Statistics Say about Diversity and Gender?

Companies will continue to face increased scrutiny over the ethnic and gender diversity of their boards post-pandemic. The number of female directors in FTSE 100 companies has increased by 50 per cent in the last five years, according to the Hampton-Alexander review. The UK-government-backed review, launched in 2016, achieved its target of 33 per cent of board positions on FTSE 100 and FTSE 250 companies to be held by women by December 2020.

The scope of this review captures over twenty-three thousand leadership roles in Britain's largest listed companies. It covers the board and extends two leadership layers below the board, making the UK's voluntary approach to improving women's representation on board, highly ambitious. The target in 2016 was 33 per cent women in leadership on boards. By 2021, the turnover rate had increased from 21 per cent in 2017 to 30 per cent in 2021.

The number of women on these boards rose from 682 to 1,026 over the five years of reporting (2016-2021), the report's authors said. The number of 'one-and-done' boards, where there is only one woman, has fallen from 116 in 2015 to just 16. However, many of these appointments are in non-executive board roles.

Data collection began in 2017. There were only four companies in the FTSE 350 that had a woman as chair and CEO – Admiral, Pennon, Severn Trent, and Direct Line. The FTSE 350 also still has twenty-eight all-male executive committees, although this is down from forty-four last year.

The explanations in 2017 for not appointing women to boards included the following (https://www.gov.uk/government/news/revealed-the-worst-explanations-for-not-appointing-women-to-ftse-company-boards):

1. 'I don't think women fit comfortably into the board environment.'
2. 'There aren't that many women with the right credentials and depth of experience to sit on the board – the issues covered are extremely complex.'
3. 'Most women don't want the hassle or pressure of sitting on a board.'
4. 'Shareholders just aren't interested in the make-up of the board, so why should we be?'
5. 'My other board colleagues wouldn't want to appoint a woman on our board.'
6. 'All the "good" women have already been snapped up.'
7. 'We have one woman already on the board, so we are done – it is someone else's turn.'
8. 'There aren't any vacancies now – if there were, I would think about appointing a woman.'
9. 'We need to build the pipeline from the bottom – there just aren't enough senior women in this sector.'
10. 'I can't just appoint a woman because I want to.'

Chair of the review, Sir Philip Hampton, echoed called to boost the number of women in top executive positions as well as non-executive roles: 'The progress has been strongest with non-executive positions on boards, but the coming years should see many more women taking top executive roles. That's what is needed to sustain the changes made.' In 2021, for his final five-year review (ftsewomen leaders.com/wp-content/uploads/2021/02/HA-REPORT-2021_FINAL.pdf), he celebrated the outstanding efforts of many FTSE 100 companies that have met or exceeded the 33 per cent target. He concludes, 'The lack of women in the boardroom is where it all started a decade ago, and it's the area of greatest progress. However, we now need to achieve the same gains for women in leadership, and indeed, more.'

Leadership is about influence. Influence is often circumstantial, influencing a group of people to achieve a goal in each situation. In the last fifty years, gender stereotypes have been increasingly challenged, and yet we still live in a world where less than a quarter of the world's managers are female, the gender pay gap in many countries is at least 20 per cent and only 1 per cent of the titled land on earth is owned by women.

Ethnic Minority Representation at Board Level

The shift from how companies used to be to how we are going to lead in the future starts at the top. Today's executives need to consider guiding their teams with shared values and a healthy culture rather than directing with rules and regulations. They must move from taking comfort in established hierarchies to embrace networked teams and work to expand their social brains. Instead of compliance, they must encourage commitment. Instead of focusing on numbers, processes, and tasks they should consider their people, quality, service, and customers. Imagine a world where leaders are authentic and unashamed of their own humanity?

Kanthi questions a company's authenticity:

'I was asked by a television production company if they could interview me and use my face as part of a film on the company. They apologised profusely for asking, but they said there were no other women or people of colour visibly available in the company.

'Although companies state publicly that they support diversity, equity, and inclusion, internally, I still found that there was a natural default toward people that look like themselves. Internal publications tend to feature white middle-aged and younger white individuals without a thought for how that would be perceived by non-white individuals in the company.

'As a business consultant, I have spent much of the last twenty years working with and interviewing companies quoted in the top five hundred on their stock exchanges in London, Dublin, New York, Mumbai, and Beijing. Rarely have I interviewed senior women in Western companies. They usually tend to be male and white. In Asia, they are invariably male and people of colour. You must dig deep into their organisations to find the diversity.'

- How authentic was the company being?
- Did they consider the impact of that request on the recipient or even their reputation?
- How well does your company demonstrate its approach to diversity, equity, and inclusion in all its publications?
- What does the tone from the top portray?
- How is the executive board in your business made up?
- How does the board operate?
- How do its members behave?

Patrick described a company he was working at:

'This was a divisional board of a FSTE 200 company that had its own organisational structure, which had control over its own resources. It was operating as a stand-alone company within the larger organisation. It had its own operational team, finance team, marketing team, sales team, but shared central services like IT.

'The board structure had a managing director, finance director, sales director, HR director, and three regional directors, of which I was one. The rest of the people on the board were white, middle-aged men apart from one middle-aged white woman who led HR. The level of experience was deep and varied, and there were no egos dominating the team.

'Yet even though I held a senior position on a board I was not party to some of the strategic discussions and subsequent decisions for some time. There were occasions when there would be discussions at board that needed more time outside of the meeting. I was not invited.'

'This sometimes meant that I would have to act on those decisions. Looking back, I could have spoken with my line manager about how I was feeling before this point to give him an opportunity to consider how this was affecting me. They could then have reconsidered making changes without including me in those conversations. However, I did not speak up. I accepted the status quo.

'Maybe if I had been more assertive, the situation would not have continued. I suppose I could have just refused to carry out the actions as I had not been involved in the decision-making process.

'At the time of these incidences, none of these options felt possible. Some of it was probably based on a lack of confidence or a fear of being accused of being oversensitive, paranoid. Worse still, I may have risked possible further exclusion.

'You see, over time from an early age, you became conditioned into not challenging, to being subservient. The last thing I wanted was to be seen as an outlier or troublesome. Things are different now.'

We will discuss speaking up, microaggressions, and psychological safety in future chapters. Suffice it to say that what Patrick was describing is a status quo which, on the one hand, was allowed to perpetuate and, on the other hand, speaks volumes about the unconscious biases present in that situation. The first collective bias, or groupthink, being the board who together determined it was OK to be selective about the areas of business in which they involved Patrick. The second was Patrick's own belief that if he challenged the status quo, something 'bad' would happen.

- How would you have addressed this situation as a board member?
- What would you have done in Patrick's shoes?

Patrick says, 'I was working in a company operating in over seventy countries with many subsidiaries, organised on a matrix management system. The business designs and delivers products and services that improve habitations and day-to-day living. From the outside world looking in, the company would appear to comply with diversity and inclusion. Company literature with glossy photos features people of colour in hard hats, in front of computer screens, or operating a piece of equipment with smiles on their faces.

'Yet when you looked for the same representation in the influential senior position, those photos were vacant. They were missing in HR documents, sales documents, and exhibition posters. If they did feature non-white colleagues, they would be shop floor workers with no representatives from administrative positions. It made me feel like I was only useful when it suited the company's agenda – perhaps to try and address something that they had been challenged on externally.'

'When I was asked to be one of the faces for the company, I disagreed with the script, because I believed it did not portray my skills, expertise, and qualifications. It was more about the colour of my skin and seemed to say, "Hey, look, we do have non-white people in senior posts."

'I felt that there was a lack of understanding of how I might feel about this token use of me. In a way, it felt patronising and hollow – there was no authenticity about what they were trying to do, and I could not accept being part of a tick box exercise.'

Interestingly, when you open UK's Parker Review on the ethnic diversity of UK Boards, this observation in the photographs of those involved and the people being portrayed rings true (https://assets.ey.com/content/dam/ey-sites/ey-com/en_uk/news/2020/02/ey-parker-review-2020-report-final.pdf).

The Parker Review was published in February 2021 by Sir John Parker, EY and the UK Government Department of Business, Energy & Industrial Strategy (BEIS). It showed that 37 per cent of FTSE 100 companies surveyed (thirty-one out of eighty-three companies) do not have any ethnic-minority representation on their boards.

Chaired by Sir John Parker and originally commissioned to consult on the ethnic diversity of UK boards, its first report was published in 2017. The review made a series of recommendations and set a target for all FTSE 100 boards to have at least one director from an ethnic-minority background by 2021. Unfortunately, it appears that the pace of progress has been slow. The review concludes that it will be challenging for FTSE 100 companies to hit the target recommendation.

Parker said: 'There is still much more work to be done to reap the undeniable benefits that diverse leadership provides. Ethnic diversity needs to be given the same level of board room focus that finally led to increasing female representation on boards.

'To remain competitive in the global market, UK businesses must focus further on the recommendations in the report, increasing alignment of the board with its customer base at home and overseas. They must also address the key challenges of recruiting board talent now and in the future, recognising the significant demographic changes taking place in the UK and international markets in favour of ethnically diverse candidates.'

Recruiting diversity onto boards starts with workforce. Companies are still overhauling their recruitment processes. Head-hunters and recruitment agencies alike are far too embedded in historical stereotypes. The one perpetuates the other and little changes.

- What are you doing about recruiting board or team members today?
- How open are you being to other peoples' experiences and points of view?
- What gets in the way of you being an authentic leader who embraces diversity, equity, and inclusion?

Patrick notes: 'There are so many images and stereotypes that reinforce myths about Black people, and some of them go back centuries. When I was a youngster, some peddled the belief that although Africans were bright and showed promise in their youth, their adult intelligence and capacity for learning waned. Nineteenth-century "scientific" racism, although not as overt as it was then, is still part of society today.

'The TV programmes of the 1970s were cruel and just reinforced the stereotype of the angry black man or woman. It was socially OK to subject minority actors to racist names and taunts because they saw it happening on TV. So, when this spilled over into the workplace, no one seemed to mind, and it was seen as good sport. Well, we did complain, but it fell on deaf ears. Who would you complain to? There was always the worry that you would be singled out as a troublemaker.

'For me, it began with the head of upper school calling by name every black boy in the class and telling us that we would come to nothing. This still rings in my ears today. It has driven me to prove that head teacher wrong.

'This attitude and mind-set of the establishment followed me into the workplace. The establishment deemed it lucky for you to get employment. You had already been pigeonholed into menial tasks that would not be overly challenging but needed to be done by someone.

'There was no difference in the treatment that the first generation of immigrants experienced. They were given jobs that the indigenous population did not want to do but that needed to be done – the menial jobs.'

<hr />

Kanthi Ford takes up her story: 'I was at university and delighted to have a summer job working in an upmarket department store on the perfumes-and-cosmetics counter. There was a sort of class system in operation in this Yorkshire city centre icon. The "posh" birds worked in perfumes-and-cosmetics while older "duchesses" worked in clothing, and working-class people worked in the basement grocery. Mainly, the full-time assistants in perfumes were aspirational air hostesses and all immaculately made up.

'It was a hot summer. The air-conditioning failed, and the staff manning the refrigerated food counters went on strike. A union representative came round and advised us that we were within our rights to refuse to stand in for other people anywhere in the store.

'That afternoon, Mrs M from HR came storming through the store. Immediately, she came up to me and said, "You will go and man the wet fish counter."

'This was my idea of purgatory, working in a boiling, smelly basement. I refused, as instructed.

'She fired me on the spot, saying, "You people are used to hot temperatures." I was so shocked that I burst into tears and was quickly surrounded by supportive perfumes-and-cosmetics assistants. The ensuing drama played out in the manager's office, and I was re-instated.'

———— ❧ ————

Patrick shared his experience: 'Earlier in my career, there was a limited expectation of me and what I was capable of – all without consulting with me. The experienced trainers I was assigned to seemed to naturally lean towards people who looked like them. They were allocated the more technical roles even when, on paper, I was equally qualified. There was no discussion, no explanation.

'The one person with similar academic qualifications to mine was white, and he landed the office job. Management roles were kept from me with no explanation. Throughout, I noticed that the management team spent more time with people who looked like them, not me. Ultimately, this made me more determined to prove what I could do.

'After I qualified, I took an interest in what the managers were doing and thought that maybe, with further training and guidance, I could eventually get a management position in the company. I sourced a course. When I went to management and asked for financial support, the answer was no. Nobody asked why I wanted to do this or sought to understand what my career aspirations were.'

———— ❧ ————

The paradigm for traditional organisations is that old boy networks should be encouraged – 'Better the people you know.' Today's companies should be actively respecting and leveraging diversity while fostering inter-dependence across teams.

- Can you see the range of biases in these accounts?
- Outline how the combination of so many small personal beliefs created a much bigger issue.
- How many boards reflect the diversity of the societies we live in?

For the first time, the 2020 Parker Review provided analysis of UK's FTSE 250 boards. They were found to be even less diverse than the FTSE

100. Of the FTSE 250 companies analysed, 69 per cent (119 out of 173 companies) have no ethnic diversity on their boards. Across the FTSE 350 (150 out of 256 companies analysed), 59 per cent have no ethnic-minority representation on their company boards.

In total, 98 out of 868 FTSE 100 directors who disclosed their ethnicity were from ethnic-minority backgrounds. In the FTSE 250, there were just 80 out of 1,503 directors and six ethnic-minority directors holding the position of Chair or CEO.

Of the FTSE 350 companies involved in the survey, 43 per cent of the ethnic-minority directors were women. So, those who were female breaks down to 41 per cent BAME directors in the FTSE100 and 45 per cent in the FTSE 250.

Kanthi enlarges on this regrettable statistic: 'Killing two birds with one stone, they used to say. I was appointed as a senior manager for a FTSE 250 company. Several people said it was convenient that I ticked multiple boxes when it came to gender and diversity. Until then I hadn't really cast myself in that mould.

'More recently, with my business hat on, I find myself consulting and coaching with board directors from FTSE 250 companies. Very rarely do I speak to senior women. It is not surprising that views become quite polarised without different voices on the board.'

Communication is everything when it comes to relationships. Companies might have the best of intentions to be equal, diverse, and inclusive, however if the board is not behaving appropriately, or telling anyone, then the effort can be diluted beyond measure. Patrick's experience highlights this outcome.

Patrick Ricketts shares his experience: 'I was delighted to have joined the business. I was the first and only person from a Black and Minority Ethnic (BAME) background in the company. Very soon afterwards, I realised the business had many challenges that if sustained would finish the company. There were orders lost in the system that had been outstanding for months, systems and processes not working, and no direction. I resolved the challenges and was recognised for this by being given a supervisory position.

'That's when the problems started. The people in the department I was to supervise were not told of this change. For a while, this was difficult, as I would agree one thing with the team only to find that what had been agreed was ignored or challenged behind my back with my line manager. I was on the verge of leaving when I decided to stand up to my manager. I made the point that I could not accept being undermined and he either had to support me or I was leaving the business.'

'It was obvious that he was struggling with telling the team that I was now their line manager because they had made it clear to him that they did not want someone like me managing them. Thankfully, he did support me.'

———— ∞∞∞ ————

- So, if you are taking a new look at how you influence others to get results, what strategies would you have adopted in this scenario?

Sustainable change takes time, but the data tells us overwhelmingly that the current pace of change is slow. The 2020 Parker Review report set out extra recommendations. These focussed on measuring board level diversity and building a pipeline of board-ready candidates.

1. Engage – FTSE 350 companies were encouraged to be proactive and report on the ethnic diversity of their boards.
2. Report – The review urged companies to report fully on their ethnic diversity policies and activities in compliance with the corporate governance code.
3. Recruit – Executive recruiters should be much more proactive in 'marketing' highly talented ethnic-minority candidates.
4. Develop – a pool of high potential, ethnic-minority leaders and senior managers.

Human Bias from Recruitment and Planning Processes

Patrick Ricketts says, 'During a lot of upheaval in my role, I had continued two nights a week at technical college for two years and gained my certificate and diploma in management. Following the successful completion of a couple of expansion projects and my recommendations for the sustainability of the larger department, the role of production manager was created. This was my moment.

'I had the experience; I had worked hard and gained the qualifications. I had successfully developed a more effective and efficient department as well as created and implemented operating standards through ISO BS5750 now ISO 9002. So, I applied for the senior role.

'I did not get an interview. The role was offered to a white, middle-aged man with no industry experience. I was given no explanation as to why I was rejected. I was gutted, felt cheated, and lost any belief that I would progress any further in this company. Finally, I left for pastures new.'

- When recruiting, how clear is your board that when it comes to diversity, equity, and inclusion, are they really considering all aspects of the culture, onboarding practices and daily norms – the behaviours accepted as currency in the business?
- How focussed are you really on shifting the organisational culture and developing new leaders of tomorrow?

Artificial intelligence(AI) is progressing in leaps and bounds. In recruitment, it asks questions of inequality in nine areas, such as diversity, equity, inclusion, communication, leadership, company policies, and practice. However, as AI becomes more widely used, it is becoming clear that the algorithms used will have been created by programmers who will inevitably have incorporated their own biases into the programming (fra. europa.eu/en/publication/2022/bias-algorithm). Never take shortcuts as to what makes a good leader without a structured process involving diversity of opinions. Otherwise, you will be open to unconscious bias in your selection criteria.

Usually, CVs are scanned as first base. Chatbot interfaces can understand differences in phrasing, regional dialects, and other types of variation. However, insufficient focus is still being placed on natural language and human understanding, and is sufficient attention being paid to behavioural nudges to stimulate improved results?

Here's a simple example from BIT David Halpern, inside the Nudge Unit, explaining initiatives to narrow the gap between white and ethnic-minority recruits into the police force. Apparently, considerable differences remained despite several changes, including an online admission exam which was marked 'blind'. The pass rate for ethnic minorities was about 30 per cent lower than that of white applicants. Multiple theories for this disparity were discussed, and finally, two of his colleagues came up with the theory that motivation and expectancies might be driving these results. They therefore added an extra line into the application which appeared immediately prior to the click-through for the test. This simply asked applicants to reflect on why they wanted to join the police and why it mattered to their community. While this made no difference to the results for white candidates, 'the ethnic-minority pass rate shot up dramatically.' It rose 'from around 40 to 60 percent, entirely eliminating the difference from white applicants' (John Halpern, *Inside the Nudge Unit*). Small changes to make a big difference.

Humans are wired to be social and to make a difference. They want to be involved and feel part of something. Asking that simple question prior to the application stimulated that thought process for the applicants. Later in this book, we discuss culture and tribal behaviours. This will share a little more of the supporting theory.

With COVID-19 seemingly exposing societal divides, minority groups believe they have been disproportionately impacted by pandemic-related restrictions. With the increase in unemployment, there will be an increase in competition for available roles. Minority candidates believe they are more likely to be overlooked in the application process. So, now is the time to redouble diversity and inclusion efforts.

What does this say about the proposed methods of countering bias? These traditional methods, such as quotas and training, can only be two-dimensional. At best, they even up the numbers or provide cross-industry insights. At worst, they create division. It's time to widen the approach.

Consider the behaviours behind a supportive culture: deep unconscious-bias awareness provides a positive and supportive environment for employers in which they can think through how to ensure that they recruit the best staff, rather than inadvertently clone themselves.

Remember: not all unconscious-bias engagement is equal. Insightful knowledge and information necessary to bring about a significant cultural shift should be part of a wider solution. Certainly, carrying out a box-ticking exercise is insufficient.

The evidence so clearly suggests that more needs to be done. Businesses will have the edge if their leadership takes the issue seriously. It is important that they maintain a critical eye when reviewing their culture and accepted behaviours as well as their succession-planning methods. Most of all, leaders must model anti-discrimination behaviours themselves.

Rational Mind versus Emotional Mind – Head or Heart?

In conclusion, as effective leaders, we must understand the way we are wired and how our behaviours and subsequent decision-making will reflect those biases. This was a recent conversation with a CEO:

'I recently took an unconscious-bias test. As a CEO, proud of my even-handed approach, I was fully expecting no bias between white or ethnically diverse people. After all, I employed a wide cross section of multi-cultural workforce and several overseas consultancies. But it was a surprise – my bias was towards white people. Worse? My bias was towards white men in the workplace. As much as that shocked me, I understood why: I've been brought up in England, was taught white history, and most of the people I worked with previously are white. I live in a leafy suburb in the West Midlands, and most of the people there are white too.

'So, it's no surprise that my subconscious mind-set – the bit that I can't control – is also white. Everyone has their own biases: if someone looks like you, you automatically feel more comfortable, and there is nothing you can do about that. Knowing that something is intellectually correct is different to the emotional, knee jerk reaction that sometimes happens."

———⊶∞∞⊷———

Bias caused by people's names is common, particularly in recruitment.

Kanthi talks about her name: 'Nobody had struggled with my first name – Kanthi or NilaKanthi – until relatively recently. Then after three years of living in Ireland, I decided to close my business and return to England to look for a new role. I was surprised to find that my name had suddenly become "foreign". Recruiters and head-hunters intimated that I would be more likely to get an interview if my name were "Kathi" rather than "Kanthi". I had wrongly assumed that in these so-called "enlightened" times, companies would have strategies to beat these classic responses to an unfamiliar name. Unfortunately, if they existed, they have not proved effective. So, I started using another of my names, "Ella". Something certainly was not going right."

———⊶∞∞⊷———

Kanthi Ford continues with another example:

'I requested a valuation of my property from an estate agent through their website. When she called, she asked to speak to Mr Ford. I said there was no Mr Ford. She then asked to speak to the "man of the house". We clarified that misunderstanding. She then said they had received this email request, but I cannot be the person who sent it as "you sound English, and the name is Asian".

'So, I countered: "I own the property, I am female, and I have an exotic name. None of these things should really have come into this discussion."'

Things to Consider

While the COVID-19 pandemic and the BLM protests have caused companies to reconsider their priorities in a business context, not all effects of the pandemic are negative. Of course, isolation has been tough for many people. Back to the amygdala, isolation causes stress. We feel more vulnerable. We become more protective. We are also missing personal interactions in and around office meetings. Interaction is happening through video conferencing, but this is not social interaction in the truest sense. So, with less personal interaction, we will fall back on stereotypes.

Remote working should ultimately be liberating and provide increased opportunity for many people, especially if they are trapped by physical location or disability. It will reduce barriers to engagement in other ways, too. How many people would have ever seen inside the homes of their colleagues before March 2020? It may have been a novelty, but it is now normal to talk to people in their kitchens, their lounges, or even the cupboard under the stairs! It should be the perfect time to encourage future diversity in the workplace and consider people who are not like you.

Define your baseline and make proactive steps to support and understand diversity in the workplace.

How well do you understand the inequities in your organisation? Draw a clear baseline in the sand before you start any new initiatives.

People and companies thrive when employees feel part of a community, somewhere they truly belong. Morale goes up. Business performance improves. To create that environment, employers need to adopt an approach which is truly holistic. Educate leaders on the benefits of a diverse workforce, identify the conscious and unconscious biases that exist in your recruitment processes, and educate your hiring managers accordingly.

Remember we are dealing with a systemic issue which is deeply embedded in society. We over-rely on shortcuts and stereotypes. The questions to ask are as follows:

- How can I continuously shift my perspective to understand others?
- How can others better understand me?

Be prepared to consider politically incorrect questions about culture, religion, and heredity. These factors frame all of us humans.

Make job postings open to a wider circulation and do not include language that may alienate a wider pool of candidates. Also, aim to interview at least one diverse candidate for every major role.

Create diversity task forces composed of a cross section of people and leaders from different departments. They should jointly examine hiring, retention, pay and promotion data.

Leaders should consider what succession planning looks like and how they can attract people from different backgrounds and ethnicity. Go to where they are, or you will perpetuate the same as you have always done.

Engage the Senior Teams!

Beware of societal stereotypes in everything you do. We tend to identify specific stereotypical traits as being those of men or women. So, the masculine cultural stereotypes are bold, competitive, adventurous, aggressive, courageous, and dominant. For women, the basic cultural stereotypes are empathic, supportive, nurturing, and community focussed.

Educate your leaders about these effects and instil wariness of their own prejudices. Encourage them to see the bigger picture and opportunities in workforce diversity. When senior leaders can see opportunity in diversity and inclusion, implementing initiatives becomes so much easier. Senior leaders could be assigned mentees from people of these diverse backgrounds. Therefore, they'd get to know them, and to understand the mentees' challenges, frustrations and general lived experiences. This would help influence thinking and decision-making at the highest level.

Once you have a baseline, make diversity and inclusion part of a wider effort, part of your company. Diversity training on its own can be counterproductive, as people may resist it. Instead, be prepared to share great stories to demonstrate the ways in which diversity and inclusion can improve your company.

Though cultures and habits across the world may vary, we are all essentially social beings. We are influenced by what others around us are doing, particularly the people we know, or feel, are people like us. Accordingly, develop communities within your culture which all work together.

Finally, be prepared for a long haul. It has taken centuries to arrive at this place. Most corporations still see diversity and inclusion as an issue to spend some time on for now, fix it, and move on. It is not enough to simply employ people from minority backgrounds. Companies need to actively engage, understand, support, and encourage continuously to make sure everyone is included. By nurturing talent, giving everyone equal opportunity to progress, everyone wins.

In this chapter, we talked about the changing business environment and the shifting role of leaders. We provided various doors and windows through which you can look to re-evaluate yourself as a leader rather than a boss. We encourage you to consider the questions in the text as well as below, to reflect upon your journey towards being a leader who is more relationship-oriented and embraces diversity, equity, and inclusion.

1. Does my organisation need to change for future success?
2. What things could be done differently?
3. What are some of the beliefs or biases that I have that are no longer appropriate for today? What can I do to shift them?
4. How can I use my awareness of the social brain to influence team members and build relationships?
5. How can I be more effective at encouraging diversity, equity, and inclusion in my area of the business?

CHAPTER 2

Be Mindful You Treat People Right

> The truth is that our finest moments are most likely to
> occur when we are feeling deeply uncomfortable, unhappy,
> or unfulfilled. For it is only in such moments, propelled by
> our discomfort, that we are likely to step out of our ruts
> and start searching for different ways or truer answers.
> – M. Scott Peck, *The Road Less Travelled*

It has been part of the social fabric over the centuries. Generations of people have liked to consider themselves superior to others, whether that be the colour of their skin, gender, or one of countless other premises. If you have never walked in their shoes, how can you understand that what you say or do may be hurtful, disrespectful, or degrading to the person subjected to it?

What goes around, comes around – or does it? Every aspect of a business is a microcosm of the wider culture. The sum of the parts equals the whole culture in its entirety. The destructive effects of miserable, demotivated, intimidated workers, arrogant leaders – or any of these other permutations in a workforce – often go unnoticed except to those immediately involved. The costs can be read in signs such as decreased productivity and increased attrition.

In the global world we now inhabit, there will inevitably be a cost to the business bottom line from limited focus on diversity, equity, and inclusion. When negative behaviours become rampant, companies can quickly deteriorate, accidents happen, litigation escalates. Yet it can be so much easier, if only people remembered the social brain we discussed in the last chapter and the importance of building relationships.

It happens all the time. People have a conversation, but no one is really listening. A meeting takes place and, especially in the online world, people are trying to multi-task. So, instead of listening and participating well, we are doing two things badly. The consequences can be considerable. Company time is taken up and simple facts must be repeated and again. Misunderstandings occur and biases can be allowed to perpetuate.

> They came over in the sixties. All the time growing up, I could hear my parents talking about the rough end of this discrimination. There were lots of discussions about the troubles they faced, but they didn't talk about people's race. They never referred to people's colour or those sorts of differences, I did not have negative influences from my parents, so I did not treat people in a negative way.
> – Patrick Ricketts

> My father came from Sri Lanka (then called Ceylon) to university in the fifties. He knew he was treated like a novelty in England. I know he experienced quite a lot of racial abuse in the UK in his various careers, but he rarely talked about it. Eventually, after a lifetime living in the UK, he came to realise that he neither fitted into British nor Singhalese (Sri Lankan) life.
> – Kanthi Ford

In the West, some issues have been heightened further by the Black Lives Matter protests. In the East, there has also been growing awareness of the importance of, at the very least, acknowledging gender and diversity in the workplace. Unfortunately, there is still a long way to go.

Many managers we talk to still differentiate the diversity, equity, and inclusion agenda from production, safety, or performance goals in the workplace. Several do not understand that feeling empathy or being genuinely curious about those they work with will develop their teams and bring about far greater engagement, motivation, and commitment from their employees.

The diversity, equity, and inclusion voyage of discovery has, in many ways, just started. The benefits of understanding the bigger picture and multiple points of view and beliefs are incalculable. Disagreements will not escalate, and work teams will feel more involved. Is not true leadership the art of moving and inspiring people towards a common goal? That means understanding the impact of other's experiences – minding how you treat others.

The ability to focus on and concentrate on the present, the here and now, is totally underrated. It is critical for enhancing efficiency and making the most of your life. With all the uncertainty that we are living through, being able to listen and engage with the present will certainly shape your future. It will enhance your performance, improve your work-life balance, and reduce stress. Being able to quieten your mind provides more perspective and greater creativity.

How mindful are you of personal interactions and what you say? Your impact can be considerable. How often in the workplace have you tried to really empathise with someone who is speaking to you? This does not mean feeling for them or sympathising with them. To be an empathic leader involves experiencing their situation with them. How often have you tried to actively enter another person's situation and understand their frame of reference, one which could be radically different from your own?

- Would you be able to understand how Patrick or Kanthi felt in these statements or stories?
- Note down how you think you would have felt.

> Through my life dealing with overt and covert racism and discrimination, the difficulty has been how to react to people perpetrating these acts about (unclear) how I feel without them seeing it as an attack on their belief systems or me being overly sensitive. Do I choose to educate people and behave in a way that I expect to be treated to influence a change in their behaviour towards me? Why can't they just accept that I am different?
> – Patrick Ricketts

As a young child I remember an adult telling me that
people who said these negative things were 'ignorant', that
they didn't know any better. Feeling superior is not great
advice. I was lucky that I did not develop into an arrogant
woman. I did grow up, however, thinking I 'knew' stuff.
– Kanthi Ford

Patrick on a bus as a child: 'Saturday mornings was always a delight for
me as it meant I was going to spend two to three hours of one-to-one time
with my mom. Ok, it was a shopping trip. However, in the week, I had to
keep an eye on my sisters, school, a bit of television, play, and bed. As my
parents worked a few jobs to keep us clothed, fed, and warm, we did not
see much of them in the week. Therefore, those few hours on a Saturday
morning in the markets were precious to me.

'On one of these Saturday mornings, we walked to the bus stop as
normal. We got on the bus, and Mom paid the fare. As we looked for a
seat, at the back of the bus, there was a young boy sitting next to a woman.
Nothing unusual in that, however, it was what he said that shocked me.

'"Look, Mummy, there's a nig-nog." His mother looked embarrassed
as she attempted to quieten her boy. What I noticed was that there was
no reaction from other white people on the bus one way or another. No
reaction from my mom either as we found a seat together and sat down.'

'I can remember feeling all these eyes from behind me burning into
my neck. I felt so uncomfortable, powerless to do or say anything, upset
and angry at the same time. Why did he think he could say something
like that? He was younger than me, no older than seven or eight years old.
Where was it coming from? From the look on his mother's face, she knew
exactly where it was coming from!

'I felt vulnerable, the fact that there was no apology from her and
no reaction from other people on the bus made me feel very alone. I was
frozen in the moment and relieved to get off that bus after what was the
longest twenty minutes bus ride I had had up to that moment in my life. I
still felt numb and somehow could not bring myself to ask my mom why
I was called that name.

'I did not speak up; I did not know at that time how to counter what
was said and did not feel that there would be any backup if I did say

anything. So, I let it slide as I did not want to be attacked or offended further.'

'This incident stayed with me for a long time. Silently, I tried to work it out. For some time, even on those Saturday mornings, I was unsure about how I would react if it happened again on the bus. It never did happen on those Saturday mornings and those feelings of vulnerability have dissipated.'

'I believe because of this experience, my behaviour towards people was starting to shape. Now I knew what it felt like to be called out or spoken to in a derogatory manner. So, I try not to offend people. It does not always work that way though, because, despite it all, I know we all have our prejudices.'

———— ∞∞ ————

- How would you empathise with and advise Patrick or Kanthi to do things differently?

———— ∞∞ ————

Psychologists refer to *fear conditioning* when something that is not at all threatening becomes so. This may be due to an association with negative beliefs or biases in someone's mind. People can get overtaken by thoughts such as the following:

- "Women can't do the job as well as a man."
- "Women will take over."
- "People of colour need constant supervision."
- "Black people are lazy."

All unfounded beliefs based on bias. The good news is that fear can fade away in time. Therefore, we would encourage organisations to consider strategically and structurally, how they can make diversity, equity, and inclusion more real, more human. After all, these beliefs and biases did not come about overnight.

Shifting beyond discrimination is a question of discussion. It needs people to get the necessary information to inform their views and comments. Above all, it requires a recognition that without all the necessary components to create a complete picture, that prejudice will remain. That is down to each one of us, and it starts early in life. We know children of colour experience racism at school.

Lewis Hamilton (Sir Lewis Carl Davidson Hamilton, MBE HonFREng, to be precise) is a world champion British racing driver. He talks of being scarred for life by racist abuse suffered as a child. In 2011, he controversially said he was being penalised by stewards 'because I am black – that's what Ali G says,' in reference to the satirical fictional television character.

His Mercedes boss, Austrian billionaire Torger Christin 'Toto' Wolff, said: 'When Lewis was young, he was the only black kid among the white kids, and I know he was racially abused on track. If that happens to an eight- or ten-year-old, it leaves scars that will not go away.'

'If as a child, you had to overcome abuse and discrimination, on one side' it makes you stronger, but on the other side, it also leaves scars. Those scars are a witness of having survived. We must acknowledge we are not very diverse in F1.'

- Have you ever considered the things from your early life which may have affected your beliefs and behaviours as an adult?
- Can you summarise all the 'big' things or life-changing events you remember in your childhood up to the age of twelve years?

Save your list until the end of this chapter. Here, Patrick and Kanthi describe some of the discrimination they experienced at school:

Patrick says, 'At school, it was considered that the black lads like me would go into apprenticeships. No one asked us what we would have liked to do. There wasn't any other way considered. If you were seen as a "good" bet, you got your opportunity. If you were seen as a bad bet, there was little encouragement. No wonder so many people ended up in gangs and on the streets.'

Kanthi details, 'My mother was in medicine, so people always assumed I was going to be a nurse, not a doctor, like my mother. At school in the UK, it was acceptable to be a person of colour and in health care, but as a female, being a doctor was perceived as a stretch.'

37

'I was bullied quite a lot throughout my school life. In the UK, girls used to pull my long black hair and say, "They've got hair like horses." The boys used to make monkey noises whenever I walked by. It felt easier in Sri Lanka, although I didn't fit there either as I was much fairer than my classmates – or so they told me.'

People who are verbally attacked may, understandably, refuse to collaborate or cooperate with those people. They may even go out of their way to avoid contact altogether. From the perspective of intelligent insight, such behaviour shows a complete ignorance of the feeling triggered in those who receive them. Inevitably it will have a destructive effect on self-confidence, and motivation. Leaders do need to be aware of the responses that can be activated in others, positive and negative.

Kanthi describes her early motherhood: 'When my children were toddlers, I used to live on the Pennines in the north of England. It was a bleak part of the world. Local people used to say that the temperature was "two overcoats colder than Manchester." That was indeed the case. Sometimes I used to go to work, dressed in boots and snow clothes, often having dug myself out of a snowdrift, to find that it had not even rained in the city.'

'Mostly, people were friendly. In fact, I have still incredibly good friends whom I met in that area. However, when I was alone in the house with my children, I was besieged by youths aged around thirteen years who used to harass me. They used to purposely kick a ball constantly for hours on end against the front door and throw stones at the windows. When I took the pushchair out, they used to shout names and make monkey noises. I decided early in this situation to ignore them. I thought they would give up. However, they became even more noisy – I am sure they were trying to get a reaction.'

'One day, as I was walking by, they spat at me. This was the final straw. That evening, when the ringleader's father came home, I summoned up all my courage and walked over to his house to request that his son and his friends desist. If not, I would call the police. That did not go well. The father then proceeded to heckle me in front of his son and the harassing continued. We moved to a new house and to a different part of the country soon afterwards.'

'This situation left me feeling vulnerable and 'different.' I was scared most of all and worried about my children if they were to grow up in such a location. It was an isolated group of youngsters, but the attitude of the parents actively condoned such behaviour.'

———— ∞∞∞ ————

Childhood memories can exacerbate the hostility between groups which hardens over generations. Early life learning can be difficult to dispel. It may be possible to change your views intellectually, but prejudice can be deep seated. The brain can also justify reality. So, for instance, if you see someone behaving unlike their perceived stereotype, the brain will rationalise that this behaviour is an exception to the rule.

Kanthi continues: 'My grandmother once said of my Sri Lankan relations: "His family are all genuinely nice, but they are different than the rest, and I know them. If people like them lived down the street, I would not want to have anything to with them."'

Research shows that diverse teams, well led, produce remarkable results. A key quality for an organisation's leader is to effectively bring together people from diverse backgrounds, cultures, and generations so that they combine best practice and knowledge. In a lot of multinational companies, people who do not speak English as their native language can be put at a disadvantage. This is a bias and not reality and is something which should, like all biases, ideally be addressed at an early age.

- As a leader, how sure are you that these things are not happening?

The shadow a leader casts spreads much further than most individuals realise. So, what we do and how we treat others is even more important than what we say. The most effective leaders are aware that their actions speak louder than words. They are their message. We all cast our shadows to influence the people around us. Think of the parents, teachers, or business leaders you have known. How many people have influenced you? Is that affecting the way you treat others?

- List the beliefs you hold or the characteristics you have which are like the influential adults in your childhood.

A company leader casts a shadow that influences the group culture. Whether they know it or not, what they do and say is reflected across the business. Sometimes, they can start to embody the business they lead. Think of Richard Branson and Virgin, Bill Gates and Apple, Mark Zuckerberg and Meta. How can a leader know what shadow he or she casts?

Awareness is key, and most leaders we meet are unaware of their own shadows. They are oblivious of the behaviours, beliefs, and attitudes they project. They would even deny the impact they have on the entire organisation. Recently, Kanthi was working with an organisation which employs a high proportion of male employees with little evident diversity in the workplace. Its performance was flatlining. When she interviewed representatives from across the business, they all talked of working faster and harder to deliver impossible targets and cutting corners to processes. There was very little effort at engaging diverse opinions or including an alternative, possibly female perspective on the situation. On further investigation, it transpired that the board was made up of white men with three women – one of whom was Asian. The CEO and board were making the decision to set the targets, and the people who knew the targets were unachievable capitulated and didn't speak up. The result was that people were working to deliver impossible targets, morale was low, more people were taking time off consistently, and attrition was high. Unfortunately, in such male-dominated organisations, the historical approach for women to succeed was to outperform their male colleagues almost repressing their intrinsically female approach to their careers.

Kanthi talks about some of the aspiring female managers she has coached over time: 'It always amazes me how quickly women can become chameleons, in a male environment. Instead of being their better self, they get stuck on being more efficient, pushier, and sometimes more Machiavellian. R was a young female engineer with huge ambition.

- Can you describe your shadow?
- How do you influence people?

The key to leading others effectively is self-awareness. Being clear about the shadow you cast will lead to greater understanding as to how and what you say impacts on others. Dynamic leaders will be out in the front, inspiring others with their vision, communicating the business requirements and motivating their people to get into action. Managers, on the other hand, do what it says on the tin – they manage people.

- What sort of shadows do you see in this work example from Patrick?

'I was relatively new to the business and was developing relationships as I travelled around the country. Building my knowledge and connections as I would need them as I progressed. I was in a meeting with two senior colleagues and one other. As I was new, I listened to what was being said after introductions. All was fine at the end of the meeting.

'It was on leaving the office and walking across the car park with one of the senior leaders that he stopped and turned to me, looking me in the eye and saying, "I don't know what you think you are doing here, what you are trying to achieve, as we don't need your kind in this business. If it were up to me, I would not have the likes of you in this business taking opportunities away from others. I will be watching you, and the moment you slip up, I will be on to you. Watch out!" He then got in his car and drove off.

'There was no one else in earshot or in sight, and although I had had things said to me before, it was nothing like this and from such a senior person within an organisation. I was stunned, frozen to the spot, not knowing how to react, so I got in my car, sat for a short while, then drove away.

'As I made my way home, my head was spinning from asking myself what had just happened to absolute anger as to why I had said nothing and then thinking about the possible consequences of anything that might have happened, should I have said something back.

To whom should I report it? Who could I rely on to support me? I expected annoyance as a new person complaining about the behaviour towards me of a senior leader when I had no evidence. I was a Black person making the complaint and had no witnesses. I was also concerned about how it might affect my future with the company and that I might be seen as a bit of a troublemaker in the making.

Also, what would happen if I came face to face with this individual again? Do I act as if nothing had happened, or would I take the opportunity to address him privately? How do I address this, confirming their biases about people like me? I felt angry, frustrated, and powerless. He was a person in power, and I was just starting my journey.

'My dilemma was, do I seek to address it and stop dead my career in this organisation, or do I walk away quietly? I chose to say nothing as I could not prove it and would just create problems for myself. I wanted to build a career. However, inside I was hurting and felt that I had let myself and people like me down. I could not even bring myself to tell anyone anything about it at the time. This experience eventually made me become very wary of people in the organisation. I found it difficult to trust people in authority for some time until I could grasp their agendas first.'

- Do you empathise with Patrick?
- What sort of shadow was his senior leader casting?
- What would you have done in Patrick's situation?
- How could he positively have changed the situation he found himself in?

The vagaries of workplace interactions can be a roller coaster. Personal attacks are not criticisms and should be acted upon. Once you have practised, it becomes easier to say, 'What do you mean by that?' or 'Have you understood the implications of what you are saying?' Most often people are unaware of their behaviours rather than implicitly aggressive. If you do not react, you are condoning poor behaviours. We are aware that this is easier said than done. If you are walking the talk and being the most authentic leader you can be, then you will be able to speak up as well as provide coaching and feedback.

Everyone thrives in environments where they feel respected and included, and believe it is safe to contribute as well as to challenge the status quo. In other words, an environment that nurtures psychological safety. If this is not possible or becomes emotionally challenging, fear will shut us down.

As a leader, ask yourself if you are creating an environment where everyone in your team feels safe to learn, safe to contribute, and safe to challenge the status quo. In the process, look around and see others with respect and fresh admiration, find deeper meaning in your relationships, and more in your own life.

Empathy is becoming a buzzword recently. As most of the world started working at home due to the COVID-19 pandemic, juggling domestic situations and work, there was an increased need for empathy from managers and leaders.

This was not a traditional requirement for business leaders. In the past, it would have meant problem solving. Today it means being able to provide advice based on really understanding the situation. Problem solving can be tempting when someone reaches out to you for support. This can make people feel unacknowledged. Instead, before they start advising, today's leaders need to be able to really understand the situation, authentically start asking questions, listen intently and only afterwards, express support.

- How many people do you know who listen intently?

High-performing leaders are empathic leaders. They have learned to put themselves in another's shoes and refine their listening skills. Listening is not just about focus on the person you are speaking to; it's also picking up the nuances of what they are saying. This can be even more challenging in a digital world where body language is not so evident, if people are wearing masks or indeed if they are trying to communicate in a second language.

How many meetings have you attended where people do not share thoughts but simply fill the next space with their own speech? How many times have you made a presentation when others are waiting to identify a gap where they can jump in?

Did you know? The human ear takes in ten million bits of information per second yet can deal consciously with only thirty bits of information in a second. Listening well means concentrating on the content and context of the conversation, not just being quiet. To be a good listener, you also must ask questions which help to clarify the matter. Finally, you will need to consider what is not being said – the verbal gestures, tone of voice, energy, or emotion with which the message is being shared. This is when communication starts. Without that involvement or engagement, people will revolve around each other rather than work with each other. This disconnect can prove of great cost to a business. Patrick and Kanthi have both experienced various personal criticisms (as opposed to constructive feedback). It is particularly difficult to know how to manage sarcasm and contempt. It can lead to the recipient feeling helpless or angry. It easily gives rise to defensive behaviours or the passive resistance that comes from feeling unfairly treated.

There has been a growing realisation in the past few years that, even if people bring prejudices to work with them, they must learn to behave as if they have none. International companies need employees who can put bias aside and appreciate people from diverse markets and multiple cultures. This will be essential for competitive advantage, something that is rarely acknowledged yet. Internal issues can be managed within an organisation. However, when dealing with external people, the dynamic can alter radically. As a leader, how you make people feel will positively motivate them and encourage improved business results.

Kanthi Ford progressed to a new environment: 'I moved from working in television to working in an advertising agency. It was an excellently run organisation. The team was diverse, multi-generational, friendly, and curious. The leadership team collaborated well with their teams and the results were excellent. Because the team was well led, the differences were perceived as an advantage. Using these different inputs, international customers engaged well with us, and we were able to deliver innovative advertising campaigns which sometimes won awards. I felt normal and in my element.'

Patrick's experience was not so rosy. He had an encounter with a customer which was to prove very different. 'I was a senior in an organisation and one of two black senior managers in the UK. This was progress. However, underlying discriminatory attitudes and behaviours still existed towards people like me, inside and outside of the business.

'A member of my team and I discussed some issues around service delivery with a major customer. My colleague believed that he would need my help to resolve this. We scoped out our solutions and agreed that we would meet with the customer to discuss the account. It was normal for the person responsible for the account to lead the meetings. I was introduced by name (not title) to the customer representative, who was very senior within their organisation. We shook hands, but he did not look directly at me. (He and I had not met before).

'We all sat down, and I listened as my colleague exchanged dialogue with the customer. After much deliberation between them, I was then brought into the discussion as it had reached a critical point where a decision had to be made on behalf of my organisation. At this point, my colleague said that as I was his line manager, I was the only one with the authority to make the decision.

'There was silence. The customer just froze. He still did not look at me. I explained the alternatives. The customer then said he had another meeting he needed to get to. It was a simple decision for the customer to make which gave his business what he wanted.

'Our customer seemed comfortable when he felt the white guy was the senior person, but when it was made clear that the black guy was the only person authorised to make the decision, it came as a shock. I don't think he could comprehend I was a leader of the multi-million-pound organisation that his company had a business relationship with and that he was going to have to work with me going forward.

'My colleague and I walked silently out of the building and into the car. After a couple of minutes, my colleague said, "I don't understand what that was all about. Do you?"

'I just said, "Sometimes people are surprised at who is in charge. At some point, I will explain." I did not know my colleague well as we had only known each other for a short time, and I was not in the mood to explain what was going on.

'It was not the first time that this had happened, although it was never as obvious as this incident. So, although I was disappointed that attitudes had not moved and a little irritated by the behaviour of the customer I was also secretly laughing because there was nothing, he could do about it – except walk away from the deal.

'Sometimes, despite the risks, you must have the courage to make a stand and hope individuals will see sense. My behaviour and my professionalism left the customer with only one thing to overcome – the colour of my skin.'

• So, how would you deal with someone from another company?

This situation occurs differently in the East. Here, there is an odd contradiction in behaviours which underlies both colonial heritage and national pride. The colonial heritage still makes people silently subservient towards white businesspeople, but behind closed doors, people of colour become brothers and sisters together.

Kanthi explains, 'I had set up a multinational consulting business in India. This example is one of many. It was a typical monsoon day in North Delhi. The heavens had opened, and the stair rod rain had temporarily ceased. It was humid and damp, very damp. In fact, we had to pick our way through the deep puddles which had grown outside the modern office block.

'I was with my country manager who was female, Vietnamese, and a Scottish male colleague. We had worked our way through the inevitable bureaucracy at the reception and were waiting to meet the Indian CEO of this multinational. Eventually, his PA, an earnest young Indian man, arrived to escort us through the building.

'We were ushered into the spacious office at the top of the building. It was luxuriously appointed with marble floors and led out onto a plant-covered balcony. The CEO walked in. He was a prominent businessperson who had also served as a member of Parliament.

'He shook hands with everyone, and as we sat down around the meeting table, he invited us to elaborate on the proposal we had prepared. As I started to explain, he turned to the man and asked that he speak instead.

'My colleague was used to this by now and politely asked, "Why?"
The answer was, "I want to hear from the boss."
'My colleague laughed and pointed to me.'

The persistence of subtle biases can explain why, ostensibly, racial attitudes towards people of colour appeared to have become more tolerant in the West. Yet more subtle forms of bias persist – people reject racism while still operating in a biased way. So, a recruiter may hire a white applicant instead of a non-white applicant because of some spurious reason, such as the former was a 'better fit' or vice versa. Maybe putting up more ethnically diverse candidates will demonstrate equality, or will it be simply tokenism?

Attracting talent from diverse backgrounds and ethnicity is assumed to be the way for a company to be considered a diverse workplace. The solution to the issue seems to be establishing and achieving a quota, or a numeric target of how many percentages of certain underrepresented groups should be hired and retained in the company. However, a diversity quota is just that – a quota.

Inclusion is not about ensuring that 10 per cent of your employees are women or non-white. It is about giving that 10 per cent a voice, including them in important meetings, and empowering them to be their best in your company. Diversity is not about only focusing on race, sexual preference, disabilities, skin colour, and gender – it is about gathering ideas from different employees, regardless of their beliefs and ethnicity. As a leader in your team, take a step back and ask yourself if you have let your employees from divergent backgrounds, gender, and ethnicity collaborate and create meaningful impacts in the organisation together. Not a lot? Then tokenism is happening in your company.

Diversity is numeric. Inclusion is cultural. Managers and leaders must create an environment where everyone feels connected and included. Encourage cross-cultural collaborations in all levels and business units. Most importantly, hire talent based on capability, not gender or ethnicity.

Symbolically recruiting a small number of people from underrepresented groups to create an appearance of racial or gender equality within the workplace or mandating that everyone must undergo diversity and inclusion training does not make a company equal, diverse, and inclusive. Tokenism creates a superficial appearance of equality without truly achieving it. It lacks the interpersonal engagement and inclusive behaviours that count. A good start would be to involve a wide range of workers in the company's decision-making process instead of just having them present as representative.

Have you ever attended a meeting or an interview where you have made your mind up about the other attendees or candidate in the first ten minutes? This normally happens because the other parties inadvertently make you notice something. It may be something as simple as a handshake or being able to share eye contact. If could be someone's appearance, gender, or colour. Either way, beware. Whether or not you make a value judgement about any of these things, the fact is that you noticed. As soon as you notice, your brain is in analytical mode and the compare/contrast/ analyse functions are switched on.

One way to overcome these innate responses is to create empathy with the others. Once you have created empathy, develop rapport and this will put you in control of the interactions. Let's take Anu, for example. She is a new psychology graduate coming for an interview. She is not smiling, looks serious, and is clearly nervous. She is wearing black trousers, with a blue blouse and blue jacket. She looks slightly smarter than the usual appearance of people in the company. As she sits down, she drops her notes because of her nerves. Would you notice? Would you like to give her the job? She has long black hair tied back and looks Indian. Did you notice? Is it more or less likely for you to offer her the job? She starts to speak, and her accent is French. Did you notice? Would it have made a difference if it were a strong Indian accent?

Of course, there are strong rules about discrimination in most organisations, but be aware how your brain might work. All of this happens in the blink of an eye, but the point is that by noticing these things it becomes harder for your brain to rise above the detail and consider holistically whether the person would fit in your organisation.

Remember: your brain is extremely cautious, so try to avoid others being hijacked by their analytical thoughts and work on your empathic skills. So, like Patrick and Kanthi, you can try to engage others in the possibility of moving beyond their first impressions.

What is the first thing someone would notice about you when meeting you for the first time? How often do you take time to introduce yourself properly and engage with them before you share your thinking? It's often what you put in that you get out.

If it is difficult to dig out these deeply held biases, it is important for company leaders as well as the individuals concerned to challenge these situations as they occur. To turn a blind eye and do nothing merely condones the behaviours and perpetuates the situation. Encourage people to speak out against even small acts of discrimination. If people keep getting away with poor behaviour, they will keep doing it and encourage the rest of their group to join in.

- Discrimination can take so many forms. What do you see in this situation?

Patrick starts his story: 'As a teenager at work with a bit of disposable income, I spent most weekends out partying. Eating was not my priority, and I would often miss the traditional family Sunday meal that my mother would have lovingly prepared for my sisters and me all day Saturday.

'This delicious traditional Jamaican Sunday meal was always rice and peas with chicken (kidney beans soaked in water and the chicken seasoned overnight). The peas were cooked with scallions, garlic and thyme amongst other spices, and the chicken was cooked in a Dutch pot.

'It would regularly become my Monday lunch at work. So, my free catalogue lime-green toastie-maker would switch on to heat up while I ran down to the shop and back for my afters and a drink. On my return, I would place my meal on the hot surfaces of the toastie-maker, chicken on one side and rice and peas on the other. The smell would flood the tool room, and there would be curious looks, some people holding noses and others enjoying the aromas.'

'One individual shouted, 'What the bloody hell is that! Where is that stuff from? Why does it smell like that? That's not chicken! That can't be chicken. Where's the Yorkshire pudding, potatoes, gravy? That's not proper food. Look at it! Is that what you are fed in the jungle? It does not look natural!'

'It was like there was only "their" type of food. This individual had been the most overtly prejudiced person I worked closely with from day one. Fortunately, by this time, I was feeling more confident about myself and more able to articulate my feeling. I was learning how to react to situations without losing people along the way.'

'So, I decided enough was enough and reacted: "Just because you only know and eat bland boiled chicken, vegetables, and potatoes boiled to within an inch of their lives, this does not give you the right to talk about my food in the way you do. I do not pass judgement on what you eat. Therefore, you have no right to disrespect my food in the way you do. If you are curious and want to talk about it, or even try a bit, then I am happy to share. Otherwise, don't air your opinions on something you have no idea about."

'He listened and took me at my word and tasted it and was appreciative. No one ever talked in bad terms about my food again. Result!'

Learning the skills to know when to speak and what to say is important. It is possible to coach people in providing feedback that is effective without causing defensiveness. Of course, traditionally, managers used to just drive for results. Most people want to know that they are making a difference, whether their work is a means to an end or an end. They also thrive when they get acknowledgement for the things they do well. So, being able to create a comfortable coaching environment for everyone will deliver results. Now managers must acknowledge the importance of providing motivation by letting people know how they are doing, that they are making a difference and are recognised.

Remember: coaching is not criticism. Often, this is a mistake leaders make. It is about being caring and supportive to provide both appreciative as well as constructive feedback. Appreciative feedback is so easy. It's surprising that it is not used more often. Letting people know what they are doing well and how much you recognise their efforts creates so much positive energy. Celebrating success delivers dividends. Equally as important is being able to signpost to people how they can improve performance. If they do not know what is expected of them or how they are failing, they will not be able to improve.

There is a distinction between coaching and feedback. Productive business relationships need constructive feedback provided in a coaching manner. Improving business performance comes through being equally balanced, using both appreciative and constructive feedback in a mutually supportive environment.

Kanthi remembers, 'I used to have a manager who would send me a spreadsheet with my performance ratings attached. If any fell below the average, he would instruct me to improve the scores, yet he would never engage with me on discussing just how or what I could improve. I was left worrying and in the dark.'

How we show up today is more important than ever before. Practising empathy also needs honesty, accountability, and hard work. Encouraging accountable behaviour by demonstrating your own accountability is key. In fact, walking the talk and leading by example are essential for today's leaders, especially when it comes to diversity, equity, and inclusion.

Key Points to Consider

- Walk the talk, lead like you are a role model, constantly on show.
- Be empathic If you hear negativity, try to see this as a personal point of view not an attack.
- Think about the impact of what you are saying.
- Be careful if you are surprised by other people's comments. Don't wrong foot yourself. Avoid an adversarial situation.
- Don't be afraid to speak up rationally to counter bias.
- Recognise people for their values. You will soon find positive benefits.
- Listen like your life may depend on it.
- Be sensitive to other's situations. You may have no idea what people's true back story is.
- Don't accept insinuation and negativity. One thoughtless comment can needlessly lead to swathes of resentment and de-motivation.
- People often say the 'right' thing. They don't necessarily behave in the right way. It is not enough to know the correct words; it is important understand their context.
- Remember: individuals are proud of their beliefs and values, so put yourself in a position where you can relate to their values.
- Giving roles in business and on the board to a percentage of female or ethnically diverse candidates is tokenism. If people are not making genuine contributions to the business decision-making, it is statistical progress alone.
- Without adequate and inclusive representation, leaders may be unaware of the issues in their business. This will lead to a false sense of security and maintain the status quo.
- Individuals selected for the wrong reasons can feel a sense of isolation and become demotivated.
- Encourage people to share stories about the things which are important to them – you will soon hear the things they value most.
- Set a big idea – don't just say that you embrace diversity, equity, and inclusion. Give your people the reasons why. Share an aspiration that everyone can buy into which sidesteps any negativity. Once

everyone owns the cause, motivation will grow, and teams will all be heading in the right direction.

- Identify what results you are driving for in your business and what behaviours you expect in delivering them.

Actions

1. Look at your list of all the 'big' things or life-changing events you remember in your childhood up to the age of twelve years. Tick the items that you see as part of your approach to the world today.
2. How many of those things remind you of a parent or teacher?
3. On a scale of 1-10, how empathic do you think you are with your peers and your team?
4. How well do you think you listen to others?
5. Think of a situation at work or at home where you don't think you have been listening like your life depends on it. What was the result? How could you have listened differently?
6. Think what diversity, equity, and inclusion means for you. Then consider some interactions at work that may need some attention – what can you say or do differently?
7. How can you describe your personal perspective on diversity, equity, and inclusion in a way which inspires and motivates others?

CHAPTER 3

Does Activism Reinforce Bias?

> I've always felt that shouty people don't do us any favours. However, as we have been writing this book, I can see a role for activism in moving the status quo.
> – Patrick Ricketts

> I believe that people are frightened by vocal activists, this in turn leads to reinforcing other people's existing biases against whatever protest they are witnessing. I see the emphasis shifting, activism, not vocal radicalism.
> – Kanthi Ford

In this chapter, we discuss company cultures and managing uncertainty as well as our evolving views on activism. Whilst we would like to explore company culture and societal influences, we believe that is a subject for others. Hopefully, by examining some aspects of corporate culture, we can start to understand the bigger societal picture, but first, let's explore activism.

Activism is ignited by change. Right now, it seems like we are in the eye of the storm everywhere we look. There is so much rapid change and uncertainty. Global pandemics, international business competition, more and more new and disruptive technologies, working from home, agile working, flexible scheduling, COVID testing as the norm. Change to the global population is happening at a pace which is faster than ever experienced before. Inevitably it is leaving people uncertain and anxious. Personal wellbeing is suffering.

Change is scary; change is hard. Leading through change is a vital leadership skill. It can be even more of a challenge if you are making a stand for diversity, equity, and inclusion. The natural human response to change or uncertainty is resistance – remember the amygdala and the way our brains are wired for survival? Most senior people underestimate the resistance to plans for change – ask any politician trying to implement a countrywide lockdown in the pandemic.

To become effective leaders, it is important to understand and anticipate resistance as well as to eliminate the barriers and biases it can create. Most people are so wired into their comfort zones, the things which are habitual and familiar to them, that having to reconfigure their worlds is almost unthinkable. This is the mind-set that leaders will have to empathise with.

Once we have discussed activism in this chapter, we will also consider why activism can reinforce bias (an own goal) or leverage change. Unfortunately, when planning to overcome resistance, companies sometimes try to enforce diversity, equity, and inclusion through introducing quotas. So, we continue to suggest ways in which more positive changes can be considered for the workplace.

Anyone who feels strongly about a cause and is working towards change could be considered an activist. Causes can be social, such as racism, gender, environmental or political issues. They tend to be supported more because of specific grievances or identities. For example, women exposed to sexism are more likely to lean towards feminism.

Both Patrick and I used to consider activism in the traditional sense – someone attending a protest, fighting for environmental and feminist issues or human rights abuses, for instance. The words we used in our discussions and descriptions of these situations included 'fighting', 'shouting for action', and 'ways to end'. In our perception, this was accompanied by strong views expressed vocally and often loudly.

Our approaches in business were less radical, more subtle. Racism and the glass ceiling for women was systematic, engrained, and widespread when we started out in our careers. Prejudices had just been there, part of our lives for as long as we could remember. So, if an activist is anyone who is fighting for change in society, why, historically, did activism appear to reinforce bias?

We can see or hope that times are changing, and negative behaviours are not being driven underground. Our children, younger people – Millennials through to Generation Z – are reshaping what it means to be an activist. Many seem to be involved in causes, but are less inclined to participate in protests, become publicly noticeable or participate in conflict. They are more social activists than vocal radicals. They appear to consider the larger picture, how they can find ways to end injustice and create communities which encourage economic, social, and psychological health. This may be the result of social media and the immediacy of information on a global basis, twenty-four hours a day. A cause for concern, though, is that, at the same time, interpersonal engagement seems to be diminishing.

- What do you feel about activism?
- How do you react to change?

Growing up in a world of National Front rallies, the Black Panther movement, and Green Peace protests, to us, it appeared that activism was about extreme groups positioning themselves in society. Existing beliefs were amplified, and biases reinforced. So, activist movements were causing polarisation of views. Both of us used to believe that rather than attending protest marches, we would work slowly, very slowly, to educate by example and overcome bias. Essentially, we were, rather too hopefully, embracing the famous Ghandi statement 'Be the change you want to see in the world'.

Patrick and Kanthi now think they were naive. They have grown to recognise that there is a place for both approaches and in accelerating change, vocal activism in the twenty-first century has a role. The rise of social media has led to issues and beliefs being aired more widely and quickly than ever before. Today, there are so many people speaking globally on the same topics that it has consequently diluted the impact of personality-led cults.

Diversity, equity, and inclusion are hardly something new. It's strange to think that, for so many, these recent years have been the first time that people have started to recognise that sexism or discrimination is such an issue. In many ways, this entire book is our small effort to share our beliefs in the value of striving for an equitable, compassionate world where racial and gender difference is understood, valued, and respected. Making our experiences known, our voices heard, we hope will continue our small efforts to affect change.

Gender equality is an old hat that's had a makeover.

Gender equality is a human rights issue which persists the world over. Most secondary school students have heard of the suffragettes. Social movements around the right for women to vote were vociferous in the late nineteenth/early twentieth centuries. Yet, in the twenty-first century, women continue struggling to have the right to education, let alone achieve support for issues such as domestic violence, assault and even pay differentials. Poverty and armed conflicts continue to exacerbate such issues. In some parts of the world, women still experience legal barriers to owning property, appropriate health care, obtaining work or being able to vote. This is not necessarily only in developing countries either.

'When I rented a house in Ireland in 2014, the contract still requested that as a single woman signing the contract, I had to obtain a countersignature from my father or brother! I refused and compromised by sharing personal financial statements instead,' said Kanthi.

Kanthi can share countless examples of unconscious bias being alive and well when it comes to women's roles in business. Here are three from different phases in her life:

- I was working in the energy sector in a relatively senior role which required me travelling across the length and breadth of the United Kingdom. The travelling was challenging, and since part of my role was to engage with the frontline workforce, some of the conversations were as well. One of the common observations I heard about any female given an engineering role was 'It's just for show 'cos she's a woman.'

- Years later, I was off-stage and preparing to make a presentation on strategic leadership in India. The energy conference was a throbbing hive of activity. Representatives from exhibition stands, anxious to show off their company's products and services, vied with representatives from businesses in the supply chain. Delegates were thronging in and around the conference hall from every corner of the globe. I looked out onto a sea of faces. There must have been around four and half thousand people sitting in the auditorium. As I walked onto stage, I heard the MC announcing my name, title, and presentation subject. Then, with one final flourish, she concluded 'and she is a woman.' In fact, we were probably the only two women at the session.

- More recently, I was at a conference in London and was having one of those coffee break conversations with someone I bumped into on the day. Jack (not his real name) was a successful managing director of a mid-sized UK company. Six foot three inches tall, he stood head and shoulders above me (I am four foot ten inches) in the busy room. I was giving him some examples of my experiences as a non-executive director and the particularly sexist comments I had received from a fellow board member along the lines of 'you women wouldn't understand these things'. Jack was surprised and concluded it must be an anomaly because 'all that stuff was sorted years ago'. How wrong he was.

The social movements around sexual harassment in the workplace, and recently the Me-Too movement have finally proved to be a force for change. Founder Tarana Burke began using the Me-Too phrase in 2006 to raise awareness of women who had been abused. In 2017, it become global currency after a tweet by Rose McGowan. She was one of the actresses who accused Hollywood producer, Harvey Weinstein, of assault in a much-publicised case in 2018.

This case and the Me-Too movement made the issue of sexual harassment in the workplace visible. This has finally encouraged businesses to adopt legal and policy frameworks and to start to put an end to it. Cynically speaking, this adoption could also be driven by share price and corporate reputation.

Movements like the Me-Too initiative have also led to popular debate in schools as well as in workplaces. It is giving rise to the dismantling of the institutions that underpin these attitudes, structures which are endemic in education, workplaces, legal systems, and even medical care.

Society's current willingness to question deeply held beliefs about sexuality, consent, and power has, in the business world (to some extent), unsettled expectations as to what is and is not deemed acceptable. Will this be the case with discrimination?

Understanding Racism

Let's get down to brass tacks and clarify what racism really is. Individual racism is a personal belief that one's race has superiority over someone else's. It is linked to racial prejudice and discriminatory behaviours, which can be an expression of implicit and explicit bias.

Institutionalised racism in a business is the habit of assigning value and allocating opportunity based on similarities. Unfortunately, gender and skin colour become easy differentiators. Racism can be expressed implicitly or explicitly. More to the point, it can be fuelled by everyone, whether they realise it or otherwise, even if they do not identify as sexist or racist. So, if the senior executives in a company are white males of a certain age, then someone who is female, or a person of colour would be 'felt' to be outside the norm and therefore not as easily accepted.

In the UK, there is a history of black activism which seems to have been overlooked by the outcry over the death of George Floyd and the Black Lives Matter movement. Most schoolchildren and adults are vaguely aware of the slave trade. Most are unaware of the campaign to abolish it or the harsh realities of those times.

Little is heard about the subjugation, life in captivity or even death of slaves at the hands of colonists. Many enslaved peoples tried to protect their lives by running away or forming communities to sabotage colonists' efforts as well as seeking legal loopholes to fight for their freedom between the sixteenth and nineteenth centuries. Sadly, little is shared of these stories in the school curriculum. Racism is treated as if it is something historical rather than applied to the attitudes and behaviours of the here and now.

In the UK, the killing of Stephen Lawrence in 1993 and the subsequent MacPherson Report in 1999 were important landmarks in heightening awareness of racism and police harassment in the UK. Unfortunately, Stephen's killers were not brought to justice until twenty years later. Meanwhile, stories of police discrimination and harassment continue in the UK and the USA.

As part of the British Commonwealth, the HMS *Empire Windrush* brought one of the first large groups of Caribbean people to work in the UK, between 1948 and 1973. The *Windrush* scandal, widely aired in the press, emerged when it was revealed that many of the people from this generation were being deported in 2017 because of flaws in the British immigration system. This situation is still being debated in the law courts.

In America, the authors of the Declaration of Independence shared a vision for a nation where justice would be equal for all. Two hundred years later, it is still yet to happen. Deep-seated systemic racism and inequalities that impact communities of colour are still woven into the fabric of American institutions.

In 2020, George Floyd, an African American, died when being arrested by four American policemen in Minneapolis. His death was played out in the public spotlight on social media as the arresting officer knelt on his neck. The subsequent outcry, the Black Lives Matter protests, and the recent trial of the policeman involved may give cause for hope that the tide may be turning, but there is a long way to go. Kanthi's experiences highlight this:

'The lack of trust for people of colour in the States is palpable. I have many stories of my experiences at the hands of US Customs and Law Enforcement officers, to share just a couple.'

'First, I will tell you about my experience after 9/11. I was working in the USA a few weeks later. It had been a successful day with a great interactive workshop with our clients. My colleague and I were travelling back to the UK and had to make an internal connection en route. I had experienced quite a lot of apparent harassment, searching, being asked extra questions, et cetera, on the journey. So, we decided an experiment was in order.

'He took one immigration desk and I another. We travelled as if we were solo travellers. My colleague made the connecting lounge an hour before I did! Why? I was stopped and searched twice as well as taken aside for further questions, and believe you me: I was the model of polite engagement.

'On another occasion, I was travelling with a friend in Florida. We were very aware of the police presence as we travelled through one of the areas of black community. It was a beautiful balmy Florida evening; we went to a café in a Hispanic community and saw the police just checking out everyone as they walked by.

'Later that evening, we drove back to our lodgings through a black community area. There were people sitting out on their front porches, music was playing, and the atmosphere was chilled. For no reason, we were pulled over by a police patrol car. The white police officer who stepped out of the car first was in his fifties and somewhat overweight. He came over to the driver's window:

'"Where are you folks off to?" he asked.

'My friend seemed wary and told me to follow his lead and "up" my English accent. He explained that I was a visitor from UK whom he had been taking on a tour, and we were just heading home. We were questioned for some time and eventually told not to stray into such areas in future. It felt scary and cast a shadow over the evening. After all, we were just going about our normal business. By the way, my friend was African American.'

- Have you ever witnessed discrimination?
- Have you ever been discriminated against?
- Have any of those experiences led you to think about some of your beliefs?

Society, Activism, and Corporate Culture

View organisational culture as a microcosm of societal culture. Broadly speaking, national culture represents the values and behaviours deemed acceptable by society in that country. Organisational culture is a company's personality. It is a combination of the shared beliefs, values and behaviours which are deemed acceptable in that business environment. In a strong culture, the energy of motivated, positive employees is almost palpable. In a weak culture, people are unaligned, human energy is dissipated, communications are fragmented, and fear and blame run rife.

As we discussed in previous chapters, fear can be a powerful emotion. Fear of differences stimulates a host of discriminatory behaviours. Fear, for many, can force caution or extreme behaviour in response to their biases. Physiologically, fear drives blood to the muscles, encouraging flight, then the brain triggers a flood of hormones that puts the body on alert and engenders an overall emotion of potential threat.

How Can You Understand Your Business Culture?

Corporate culture combines organisational values with shared beliefs and behaviours. Values will be the things that a company determines is important for the business. They are invisible, however, and will be determined by how they are interpreted – by the things that company executives say is important – and the way people do things at work. There will be unwritten ground rules. Additionally, certain people and activities will be praised more than others. The visible elements of culture in a company or, indeed, society, are policies, systems, laws, and stories which celebrate specific behaviours. Understanding your culture is like acknowledging gravity. It is all around you, but you cannot see it. It affects you every day, but people rarely acknowledge it.

• What do you think of the company cultures in the following quotations?

Patrick says, 'My dilemma when first in business: how to have my authority respected by people who were subordinates and peers while retaining credibility with my white middle-aged superiors.

'One way, I felt like I had sold out; the other way I ran the risk of being dismissed as management material. All I knew was, you cannot act in a combative or angry way if you want to influence change. All I wanted to achieve was to rise to a position in the hierarchy where I could influence change.'

'My first career was in the media. Attitudes were varied, but there were strong sexist and racist overtones. Earlier in this book, I described the head of HR advising me to 'sleep my way into a better role'. There were countless senior male colleagues who used to hit on me because they felt they could. I felt insignificant.' Kanthi.

'When I worked in television, I had the precursor to today's trolls – racist letters that arrived through the post. I was shocked one day when a black colleague received a letter with a cartoon of himself in a hangman's noose! He was very shaken. We all were. The company told him to ignore it.' Kanthi

"If You Do It, We Can't Be Accused of Being Racists" (Part One)

Patrick's Story

'There were some performance challenges at one of the southern factories, and it was agreed that a respected colleague from one of our high-performing northern factories would spend some time there. Their role was to understand the challenges and then support the southern team by showing and then helping them to implement procedures and best practices that were known to work successfully. Initially, this was all going well. All was confirmed by the local team and the senior manager responsible for the location.

'Later, I heard that there had been an incident in the office and that our colleague from the north had been suspended pending an investigation. I had heard that there was some friendly banter between colleagues in the office, and something our northern colleague had said had offended our southern colleagues.

'I was asked if I would conduct the interviews on behalf of the company as part of the grievance process. The company knew that I had conducted these processes effectively before. Also, because I was black, the company believed that I would not be accused of any bias if the grievance was not upheld.'

'I had spent some time in the company of the office staff in the southern factory, and I knew they looked at me as part of the establishment. My accent was "posh". I just spoke differently.'

'In our conversations, they would hang on every word, always looking to catch you out – were you proud of being black or subservient to white people? What they used to call an "Uncle Tom". To be clear, Uncle Tom was the title character of Harriet Beecher Stowe's novel *Uncle Tom's Cabin*. In this novel, an enslaved African American man (Tom) is beaten to death by a cruel master for refusing to betray the whereabouts of two other enslaved people.

'Anyhow, back to the disciplinary hearing, I considered the request for some time. Personally, I felt it was a bit of a hot potato. The incident involved an apparently racist comment from someone representing the white establishment. There was also a militant black woman with a history of radical activism who was looking to make someone pay heavily for an unacceptable remark. I would be stuck in the middle. Was this an opportunity for me to make right so many historical wrongs for my race by upholding the grievance? What would be the impact for me if I conducted the process in my usual fair and unbiased manner?

'I felt that I was going to be used by the company for reasons I was uncomfortable with. It was clumsy and patronising, a step too far. I did not want to be labelled one way or the other and felt that I would be compromised whichever option I took. It would destroy all that I had worked to build over many years. Ultimately, the approach was short-sighted and might have created more division. So I explained my reasons and declined.

'Very few people knew of my dilemma. As far as I am aware, it stayed that way, and the company respected my decision. It did leave them with an issue to resolve. This was also my way of protesting that businesses cannot continue to have tokenism. I thought that it would not happen again. How naive was I!

'One thing I have never wanted to lose is my identity as a black man and the connection with my race. I also accept that there will be a degree of "blending", and that is a constant struggle for me. You cannot keep harking back to the past, but know your history and use that in the right way to influence the future state, not to behave as if it is still the 1970s.

Kanthi continues, 'In one of my senior roles, the company was producing an internal video to promote diversity and inclusion. The only problem at that time was that there was little diversity or inclusion. The camera crew and producer spent some weeks travelling around office locations seeking visual representation of the company aspiration but literally came up with four people of colour doing different roles (from seventeen thousand) and only one woman. I was asked if I minded being filmed to add to the balance.

'I agreed as I believed that the company genuinely wanted to change and by people seeing a woman of colour in a senior role, it would encourage a different perspective.'

These quotations provide a range of business situations and behaviours.

- Can you list some company beliefs and behaviours that perpetuate discrimination?

So, what clues would we recommend in identifying your company's culture? Of course, some measurements of culture are attributable to industry and environment, organisational history, current senior executives, types of employees and locational differences.

We suggest considering the tone from the top of the organisation – what the leaders say – is an essential indicator. Secondly, we observe the combination of behaviours that the senior team display, what they do, and whether it reflects what they say. Are they coaches or old-style hierarchical bosses? Do they look at productivity outcomes based on company values, or do they celebrate productivity and commercial success, at any cost?

A third indicator of culture is the behaviour of the people in the organisation. Are people engaged, energised and supportive, or are they dismissive, critical, and negative? Do they seek to encourage others or find blame?

Fourth, try to understand the company approach to policy, procedures, and targets. See if the aspiration for everything the company does is itemised in minutiae and risk and governance rules. If so, the company is probably culturally immature.

Finally, look at the subjects which get attention in meetings. If most of the conversation is about productivity and costs instead of other cultural drivers such as diversity, equity, and inclusion or health, safety, and wellbeing, then you probably have more of a process-driven culture.

There are several models of cultural assessment available in the market. Boutique consultancy Tribe Culture Change (www.Tribecc.com) has developed a cultural maturity model based around health, safety, environment, and wellbeing (HSEW). They have a track record for providing baseline culture assessments and using nudge techniques for companies that are embarking on a cultural transformation.

Talking of tribes, I would like to speak about organisational culture and the context of tribal leadership. This has been the lifetime's work of a colleague, John King, who has some interesting perspectives on the application of cultures and how leadership behaviours drive bias as well as change. John's *New York Times* bestselling book *Tribal Leadership* was first published in 2008. He has used its concepts in countries around the world and is currently working extensively in the Middle East.

Fundamentally, in John's tribal leadership thinking, every organisation comprises a group of small towns, all with their own communities. Each community forms a tribe with its own dominant culture. Any group of 20-150 people is a tribe, and groups of people larger than 150 tend to form multiple tribes. Tribal leadership is made up of five stages. Stage one, the lowest level, is thankfully rare, with only 2 per cent of companies representing this stage. Stage five, the top, highest performing level, is equally rare.

Stages of Cultural Interaction
(Adapted by Kanthi)

Stage	Mood	Theme	Focus	Tell-Tale Signs
5	Wonderment	'Life is great.'	Team	Focus on limitless potential
4	Tribal pride	'We're great.' (And they're not.)	Stable partnership	Common purpose 'we' not 'me' language
3	Lone warrior / silver-backed gorilla	'I'm great.' (And you're not.)	Personal domination	Knowledge is power 'I' not 'we' language
2	Victim	'My life is not good.'	Separate	Detachment
1	Despairing hostility	'Life is not good.'	Alienated	Despair

Stage two is significantly different from stage one. Although apparently similar, these two stages are worlds apart. Stage one could be the workplace equivalent of a neighbourhood terrorised by street gangs, so would drive the opposite of diversity, equity, and inclusion.

Stage two is where individuals are isolated, activities are carried out in silos and people feel uncomfortable and detached. Common signs of stage two behaviours include apathy or separation from organisational concerns; resignation (effort doesn't matter, and not trying is the best option); passive-aggressive behaviour, especially toward leadership and organisational initiatives. Finally, conversations frequently involve complaints. In stage one and stage two, division is inevitable, and inclusion is rare. Stage two and stage three need each other.

Stage three is marked by an attitude of 'I'm great, and you're not'. Notice how this approach also ensures and requires a stage-two person or group to exist. There is almost a Master-Servant dependency. In a stage three culture, knowledge is power. People in stage three have an approach of superiority and entitlement. In this arena, biases will thrive.

Common signs of stage three people are that they focus on themselves and like to appear cleverer or better than others. Their actions emphasise personal interests. Individuals form dyads rather than triads (two-person vs three-person relationships) and may avoid bringing people together.

People resist sharing information with others and find validation in being better informed than others. At the end of the day, for people at stage three, winning is the only thing that matters, and winning is personal, not inclusive.

Meanwhile, those in Stage Two may be co-dependent with other Stage Two people but they also can see what drives people in Stage Three. This provides them with an insight into the fallibility of entitlement. These stages also underpin some of the racial tensions we have been describing. It is that sense of entitlement that gives rise to those unfortunate experiences we described. It is that sense of privilege which reinforces those unconscious biases around superiority.

The five stages can be found today in individuals and organisations around the world. If organisations could aspire to stage four behaviours, then its people would be displaying behaviours commensurate with a 'Together we're great' mind-set – diversity, equity, and inclusion would be a given.

Upgrading your organisational tribes from stage one to stage four and beyond yields top performance from employees, enables the organisation to attract and retain top talent and, above all, creates an environment for richly diverse culture.

So, in summary, if prejudices are a variety of unconscious biases and emotional learnings, then it is possible to win the hearts and minds of your people by developing individuals into motivated groups, all working together for one purpose. This is learned behaviour. It will take time to undo old habits and introduce new ones. It will not be fixed by a one-off diversity workshop. What can change the dynamic, though, is to motivate your people towards a common purpose with sustained efforts to involve people from different genders and backgrounds. Stereotypes can break down if people learn to work together.

- What sort of culture and leadership behaviours do the following companies have?

Patrick's story continues:

If You Do It, We Can't Be Accused of Being Racists (Part Two)

'Moving on, a few years later, I had become a senior director responsible for hundreds of employees and hundreds of thousands of customers across the country. One of the business units was in year-on-year decline. The senior manager had been there for a long time and was politically adept as well able to navigate any pressure from his line managers. We were called to a restructuring meeting, and it was announced that I would be assuming responsibility for this location. My first thoughts were *Why me, why now, and what's the fit?* This was even before I considered why no one had consulted me first.

'No substantive reasons for my appointment were given to me at the time, and I had no briefing at any point. I was at the stage where I was keen to grow my portfolio and reputation as an effective leader, so, I just got on with it.

'As the weeks went by, I began to unearth all kinds of issues. I talked to one of my colleagues about the challenges I found on many occasions. As he was the previous person responsible for this location, he was aware of the problems.

'During one of these conversations, I suggested that the manager needed replacing. He answered that they had attempted to do this more than once and, on every occasion, the race card was used. This meant that he used claims of racial bias and unfair dismissal to argue his case to remain. My colleague then concluded that if I did, we cannot be accused of being racist.

'I felt that the company had not learned anything. I mistakenly assumed that I was given this location because of my proven ability to listen, understand and support people to improve their personal performance. The comment made by my colleague really irritated me. It was a selfish and cowardly way for the company to pass off their problem, should there any claims made of racial discrimination if it went pear-shaped.

'This gave rise to a whole raft of personal questions: How do I deal with it? What could I accuse the company of? Where would the support come from? What would be the result of any grievance I put forward? What were the consequences of winning or losing? I concluded my position would have become untenable. If I won, career progression would stall. Lose, and I could not stay.

'Later, I decided that that I must let it be known that I could no longer be treated in this way. Hopefully, it was my way of starting to influence the board's thinking before they made any future decisions.'

'The board consisted of one middle-aged white woman, one middle-aged black man, and six white middle-aged men. It was decided that this executive needed some diversity training. At the time, there was legislative pressure for recognising women in senior roles. If time allowed, race and inclusivity would be discussed.

'The evening leading up to the session followed the usual pattern. We would get together for an evening meal, drinks, and informal conversation. One of the middle-aged white men, knowing that we would be attending the diversity session next day, seemed hell-bent on sharing all his opinions before the morning.

'At dinner I was two seats away to his left. He was holding court. He had been talking in demeaning terms about people that pulled rickshaws when he then without hesitating said the word *wog*. When challenged, he repeated it with a bullish expression. I looked directly at all the other members in my line of sight. Some looked embarrassed, others looked down, but not one of them said anything.

'Later, in the bar, I asked why was I the only one that called him out? I could not believe that we represented nearly two thousand employees of different ethnicities, and everyone stayed silent.

'In the morning, we gathered for the session and before the external company delivering the diversity session was allowed into the room, our senior exec addressed the group to say that some of the things said were not appropriate and that we must *all* be mindful of what we say in future, as it will not be tolerated.

'From that moment, any respect I had left for some of the senior people had gone. I decided I would stand up for what I believed in and would go further to use my senior position to champion those who would not have the help of the hierarchy because they did not look like them or come from the same background.'

<hr>

Kanthi responds:

'Being assertive is difficult in these matters. I usually find the better solution is to make the point by making light of it. As a child, I was often reminded of that old saying, "Sticks and stones may break my bones, but words will never hurt me." As I got older, I recognised that ignoring feminist or racist comments gave them room to breathe and grow – become institutionalised. So, what happens for people who have no confidence to speak up for themselves?'

Now that organisations are more aware about issues of sexism, initiatives to embed diversity and inclusion as core to their businesses have become the norm. There seems to be little effort to engage people with understanding the deep-seated beliefs which may be affecting their approach. In short, there will be a whole generation of workers who will have diversity, equity, and inclusion computer-based training who will have not experienced any deep-seated personal questioning or learning. They will have been through an electronic or face-to-face sheep dip that signifies little. Nonetheless, companies will claim to have implanted diversity, equity, and inclusion as part of their values. Box ticked. Nothing will change.

Diversity, equity, and inclusion, DEI, has become the acronym of the century. Every company seems to be implementing diversity, equity, and inclusion initiatives within their organisations in hopes of a more favourable public image and maintaining their share prices. 'We don't want protestors with Black Lives Matters placards in our lobby.'

Shared values are the key to high-performing teams. Clearly stated, accepted, and lived, they will become the guiding principles which set the guidelines for day-to-day behaviour. Doing the right thing becomes second nature. If an organisation behaves in a way, that does not reflect its values, it is lacking both integrity and alignment.

Ethics and integrity form the basis for all high-performing cultures. This implies a congruence between words and deeds. It is not an easy task and takes years of determined commitment by a company's leaders to ensure it moves forward. If leaders are to change a culture, everyone must become acutely aware of who they are (self-awareness) and what they do, and the message that communicates.

In the past, activism against racism didn't make people feel they could change the system. Now, the Black Lives Matter movement, which was causally related to higher levels of perceived inequality, higher feelings of ownership, and more action aimed at changing the relevant systems, has increased pressure on organisational cultures to encourage inclusion, diversity, and equality.

In conclusion, our view is that, nowadays, activism does not necessarily reinforce bias. Rather, if it triggers empathy, it can raise awareness of bias. We have talked about and shared a few of our experiences of gender discrimination and racism of three different types – individual, cultural, and institutional.

Individual includes specific or personal targeting. Cultural is embedded in societal norms such as media representation or employment. Institutional is embedded in policies, behaviours and attitudes encountered in established businesses and other institutions such as visibility of diversity on company boards, or police behaviours.

We have suggested that certain conditions are making it difficult for women or people of colour to achieve senior roles in business. So, instead of serving a platter of solutions to either gender discrimination or racism, we have attempted to highlight some examples and impacts of bias. In this process, we would like to think that we could raise future business leaders' accountability for their behaviours and subsequent business cultures.

It is great that we are starting to see active initiatives for greater inclusion. For instance, Google with its highly diverse global workforce, has recently announced that it will be linking senior executive pay to diversity and environment goals This was predicated by a 2020 US diversity report that black and Latin extraction people account for only 7.9 per cent of Google's workforce. Unfortunately, without holding a mirror up to leadership behaviours and decision-making processes, as previously stated, all too often initiatives like this can become an exercise in ticking boxes and achieving measures rather than shifting behaviours.

We hope that hearing our personal stories can demonstrate the implications of sexual discrimination or racism. Company boards remain unrepresentative of a multi-cultural society, with limited diversity. Policies for DEI do not guarantee structural change. Theatres, museums, and other arts facilities as well as films and television programmes also need greater visible representation for diversity. People from a range of ethnicities must be employed in such endeavours and actively encouraged to speak up and participate in the community. Even when people bring prejudices to work with them, they must understand that they should behave as if there were none.

- Is there a place for activism in the twenty-first century?
- What are my personal values when it comes to diversity, inclusion, and equality?
- What are my company's shared values?
- Do the company's values reflect my personal values?
- Where am I as a leader in tribal culture?
- What sort of tone do I set? What do I ask, and how do I behave?
- What cultural barriers to diversity, equity, and inclusion do I see in my organisation?

CHAPTER 4

Streets or Establishment?

Other kids were into Superheroes; I wanted my superpower to be world-class maths ability. My schoolteacher told me I looked like Mohammad Ali and should be a boxer. I accepted that.'

People of my age trusted teachers more than their parents.... My parents told me I could be the best mathematician in the world. They encouraged me to be the mathematician I could be.
– Nira Cyril Chamberlain, OBE CMath, British mathematician

In a traditional Asian family, to be successful you were expected to go into one of three professions – doctor, lawyer, or accountant. Anything else was deemed failure. In the UK, my family pressure was more about succeeding as a woman in a man's world. I was lucky. My English grandmother was enthralled by television. She thought I would be a great television producer; it gave me the confidence to aim for the role. If only I knew then, what I know now.
– Kanthi

It was a tough call. My school mates couldn't get it. Why did I want a proper job rather than hanging out? My teachers dismissed my ambition – limited as it was in those days. It caused so many internal conflicts – would I lose my identity as a black man? Would I belong nowhere? How would I overcome it? Peer pressure is powerful.

– Patrick

In this chapter, we explore the need for vision, both for personal development as well as for changes in business and in society. We also highlight our personal experiences of systemic racism in the community and in education, in the hope that evidence like this may identify the barriers facing some young people and signpost the resources that can be used to overcome these difficulties. The chapter concludes by suggesting that in the workplace, there needs to be more focus on a vision for inclusion and equality supported by dynamic new starter and apprentice programmes with the potential to raise the bar for inclusion and diversity in the workplace.

Vision is the compelling force that activates the drive, energy, and creativity needed to shift culture. Visons which excite have empowered humans throughout history. They can be shared through personal stories like Malala Yousafzai. This young Pakistani activist for female education is a Nobel Peace Prize laureate. Aged around eleven, she wrote a blog under a pseudonym describing life under the Taliban. She also championed the rights to an education for girls and women and was nominated for the Children's Peace Prize by Archbishop Desmond Tutu.

Visions can be illustrated in religious stories, like the biblical Moses parting the Red Sea, or in presidential objectives, such as John F. Kennedy's speech from 1962 that began the program to launch a man to the moon and back. A vision can be a single cause around which people gather to declare their truth: 'India will be free' (Mahatma Ghandi on creating an independent India) or Martin Luther King's 'I have a dream that my four little children will one day live in a nation where they will not be judged by the colour of their skin, but by the content of their character'. Visions can set the direction for a company. Steve Jobs's vision of a 'computer for the rest of us' sparked the PC revolution and made Apple an icon of American business. 'To accelerate the world's transition to sustainable energy' from Tesla, the electric car company, to Amazon's 'to be the Earth's most customer-centric company, where customers can find and discover anything they might want to buy online,' they all set the direction so that people can see where they are heading, whether within a company or externally.

Visions can encompass personal dreams and help to signpost to your future. Whatever it may be, a vision is an essential ingredient of success for people, teams, companies, countries. We can all remember the moment when our visions became real – whether it was at home, at school or transforming a business. Expressed clearly, it is motivating, inspiring, energising. It is a simple description of our aspirational future. It pulls people together and provides them with a common goal. It is our why for action. So it is essential that leaders speak in a way that others want to listen to and stay engaged with.

Every single organisation knows what they do, and most companies know how they do it. Many organisations do not know why they do it – what is their purpose, unifying cause and belief. Inspired leaders, regardless of their role, actively start with why? Mission and strategy spell out the how and the what. A compelling vision will motivate. The lack of vision will confuse and divide people. So how can a vision relate to a societal shift towards inclusion and equity?

A vision is the reason why people and companies are so successful, or why Martin Luther King inspired such a following or why Charles Lindbergh flew across the Atlantic. Company leaders, or leaders like President John Kennedy or Martin Luther King, all think, act, and communicate in the same way, which differentiates them from other leaders.

- What is the vision for your business?
- Does your business have a vision for diversity, equity, and inclusion in the workplace?

Inclusivity is concerned with the identification and removal of barriers. It involves collecting, collating, and evaluating information from a wide variety of sources to plan for improvements in policy and practice. It is also about using evidence of various kinds to stimulate creativity and problem solving.

If you believe that inclusivity is a basic human right and the foundation for a more just society, then more effort is needed to remove social exclusion arising from discrimination about race, social class, ethnicity, religion, gender, and ability. The dilemma for us all is that social categorisations, such as race, class, and gender, lead to discriminatory processes. They dilute the vision.

The extent to which peoples' experiences are inclusive and equitable depends on a whole range of interacting processes that reach into the workplace from outside. These include the demographics of the areas served by the business, the histories and cultures of the populations who work there, and the economic and social realities faced by those populations.

Patrick highlights examples of barriers to inclusion that he experienced. These include intentional attitudes such as isolation or bullying combined with unintentional attitudes arising from lack of knowledge and general awareness.

- What barriers and behaviours do you see in the following story from Patrick?

'I was determined to lift myself out of the community I was living in,' Patrick explains. 'There was a propensity for some members of all groups in that neighbourhood to rely on the state to look after them. This did not sit with my dreams of what my adult life would be like.

'I did not want to rely on anyone for my living and that meant getting a trade, an apprenticeship would be the course I would go for. At the time I never spoke to anyone about it, it was just something I believed I needed to do. I had observed my parent's generation. They struggled. Although hard-working people who toiled for everything they had, they could not pull themselves out of these communities.'

'As part of the school leaving process, you would have a session with a career advisor. I entered the room excited about what I was going to say to the advisor. I knew I wanted to be a mechanical or electrical engineer.

'The advisor said, "Well, we will do what we can for you."

'I thought, *Right, that's it, I am on my way; they are going to find the career I was looking for.* I was so excited. I was determined to land the right type of job, and this could be it.

'Later I got a call from the careers centre. They had something for me working in an electrical company. I thought an apprenticeship. I was told that I would be assembling products on a production line. My head was spinning with a multitude of questions: *How am I going to get what I want? Was it me, my qualifications, or a report from the school?*

'I had ringing in my ears what I, and other boys that looked like me, had been told: "You will not come to anything," which made me even angrier. I felt like everybody was against me. I had no idea who was I going to turn to for help. I felt deflated and lost. After some reflection, I became more determined to prove them all wrong. Instead, I started applying for jobs and apprenticeships and secured a craft-engineering apprenticeship with a family firm.

'I was so pleased I told anyone that would listen. On one occasion, I was in the centre of town and met up with a few mates. I told them with great joy that I had landed an apprenticeship.

The response from one of them was, "Why do you want to go and do white man's work? That's not for us, is it?"

'This was the first time that I had heard this from anyone. Why would he think like that? I even felt embarrassed that I had told him my news. He was an influential guy; how would this affect my standing with our group? Until then, I naively thought that everyone wanted to do well and get off the streets.'

- How many aspirational young men and women do you think fall at this first hurdle?
- What does it take for them to realise that they must be resilient and find their own way?

Patrick continues: 'On reflection, I often wonder what would have happened if I had not made it out of that situation. What if I had allowed my peer group to pressure me into being just like them in mind-set and behaviours? It was not far removed from some of the people that came over in the '50s, '60s, and, indeed, what I still hear today in barbershop discussions.

'Both experiences knocked me back and left me to reflect on which direction to take. I had choices. I could stay with my friends and acquaintances and follow the same path. I could accept what I had been told by people that didn't have my interests at heart. I decided to follow my path and have been doing that ever since.'

It is inevitable that these educational experiences will convert into the workplace. The first barrier to success lies with workplaces genuinely fostering diversity, equity, and inclusion. As described before, it needs a simple, energising vision of the why for being a fully inclusive, diverse, and equitable company. These companies will develop cultures which encourage their workforces to value diversity as it appears on many levels. Their people will also be representative of the diversity that they are seeking to embrace as well as understanding the differences between the concepts of *integration* and *inclusion*.

- How big was your personal shift when you left education and entered the workplace?
- Do you remember your first day at your first job? Can you remember what you felt and thought?
- What questions were you asked?

Kanthi explains, 'I used to wear saris for special occasions, but I stopped as I got fed up with people asking the sort of questions which made me feel like an outsider.'

Patrick was also challenged by his peer group and the clothes they were wearing. The style at the time was driven by the Jamaican music culture of the '70s and '80s, whether that was dancehall or reggae music or even religion (Rastafarianism). It was also led by how the prominent artists dressed and what the people in Jamaica who followed them were wearing, and living their lives. They influenced the dress code and way of life of many UK Afro-Caribbean men and women of my age group and beyond.

Some men would wear elements of military fatigues, or trilbies, pork pie, and baker boy hats worn with bright-coloured clothing that identified with the musical stars of the time, including, for some, dreadlocks topped off with red, gold, and green hats that freaked out the establishment who were stuck in the more conservative dress style of post-war Britain.

Patrick continues. 'As I continued my chosen path it became increasingly challenging to mix with people that looked like me. The type of clothing "uniform" that many males of my race were wearing was sometimes treated with suspicion and disdain by the establishment. It was not conventional, and where first impressions count, it was not going to do you any favours in getting on.

'I was proud of how my people wanted to identify. However, as someone that wanted to get on, I knew that I would have to go in a different direction, and as I was always more comfortable in tailored trousers, shirts, and shoes in less flamboyant colours, I continued down the route which was more acceptable to the establishment.'

'Yes, it sounds terrible, but it's true – on reflection, I assimilated. It felt terrible because that's how you had become conditioned within your community and amongst your peer group that looked like you. However, I did not see it as selling out but as getting on with my life the way that I wanted to, therefore, on reflection, some assimilation was probably necessary. So, I had started to dress differently (influenced partly by the image I wanted to portray at work). What also became more of a challenge for me was the language being used in some sections of the black community. The people that I would choose to spend time with outside the workplace were different and the way I spoke had started to change because of the environment I worked in.'

'Some of the people I worked with became my friends. The contact I had with my old school friends that were black and Asian was diminishing. So, I found it a challenge sometimes to interact credibly. I also believed that some of the language used was to test my 'blackness'. Was I still one of them? Or was I now a 'coconut' – black on the outside and white on the inside?'

'I knew that I would never forget where I came from, despite the implied mutterings of some of my peer group. I knew which direction I had to choose to achieve my goals and continue my path regardless of whom I might leave behind. It made me stronger, more determined, and resilient.'

Patrick felt like the filling in a sandwich. The workplace was not always a welcoming place, and his peer network treated him with suspicion. He was in a neutral zone. Unless these experiences are understood by leaders of organisations, they will not be able to make the necessary changes in their organisations to support inclusivity at all levels.

- How much empathy do you have with the people in your work teams?

Both Patrick and Kanthi were lucky. Their childhoods had enabled them to develop personal visions. It is important for everyone to have a personal vision. So, consider the elements that will motivate. There are just a few universal themes that activate personal buttons. The first is to make a difference. The second is to add value to others. The third is to be the best, be a winner, be part of a winning team.

- Do you have a personal vision? Try and write down what you believe is your purpose.
- How would you like to show up as an inclusive leader?

Usually, the onus is placed on employees to adapt to the work environment and the needs of the business. Inclusive cultures fundamentally create environments where all colleagues can be successful regardless of role. With inclusive workplace cultures, there will be a strong need to structure the environment to foster a sense of belonging and hospitality. This often requires a shift in attitudes on the part of business leaders, colleagues, and all recruiters.

Another barrier to inclusive workplaces is the basic lack of knowledge and skills to effectively implement inclusivity. There is a lot of well-meaning decision taking – the wrong decisions for the right reasons. The recent heightened publicity about diversity, equity, and inclusion has meant considerable attention from businesses. However, we fear much of this is cosmetic with minimal interest in, or understanding of, true inclusivity. Without a vision for inclusivity, initiatives will peter out.

From a systems perspective, having leaders who do not feel they have the knowledge and skills necessary to effectively lead diverse workforces in inclusive teams, creates an inevitable barrier to the implementation of inclusive business practices. In turn, this will create pressure to abdicate the responsibility to others.

Symbolically recruiting a small number of people from underrepresented groups to create an appearance of racial or gender equality within the workplace or mandating that everyone must undergo diversity and inclusion training, does not solve the dilemma. Tokenism creates a superficial appearance of equality without truly achieving it. It lacks the interpersonal engagement and inclusive behaviours that count. A good start would be to involve a wide range of workers in the company's decision-making process instead of just having them present as representative.

Inclusion is not about ensuring that 10 per cent of your employees are women or non-white. It is about giving that 10 per cent a voice to be heard, including them in important meetings, and empowering them to be their best in your company. Diversity is not just about focusing on race, sexual orientation, disabilities, skin colour, and gender – it is about gathering ideas from different employees, regardless of their beliefs and ethnicity. As a leader in your team, take a step back and ask yourself if have you let your employees from different backgrounds, gender, and ethnicity collaborate and create a meaningful impact in the organisation together? Not a lot? Then tokenism is happening in your company.

Martin Luther King, Nelson Mandela, and Desmond Tutu all had visions for inclusivity, advocated action, and lived their beliefs. Their nonviolent protests over existing conditions changed the world as we know it. The lack of adequate and appropriate accountability mechanisms also gets in the way of inclusive workplaces. The need for accountability relating to the implementation of inclusive workplace cultures is crucial. Systemically, the lack of accountability over the years has helped to contribute to workplaces with limited diversity, with inconsistent implementation of inclusive models.

We will discuss accountability more in chapter five. It is appropriate here to remind you of some of the concepts we discussed in earlier chapters, 'Unconscious Bias and the Brain'.

- Have you ever attended a meeting or an interview when you have made your mind up about the other attendees or candidate in the first ten minutes?

This normally happens because the other parties inadvertently make you notice something. It is something as simple as a handshake or being able to share eye contact. If could be someone's appearance, gender, or colour. Either way, beware. Whether or not you make a value judgement about any of these things, the fact is that you noticed. As soon as you notice, your brain is in analytical mode and the compare-contrast-analyse functions are switched on. One way, to overcome these innate responses is to create empathy with the others. Once you have created empathy, you can develop rapport, and this will put you in control of the interactions.

Of course, there are strong rules about discrimination in most organisations, but be aware how your brain might work. All of this happens in the blink of an eye, but the point is that by noticing these things it becomes harder for your brain to rise above the detail and consider holistically whether the person would fit in your organisation. Remember: your brain is extremely cautious so try to avoid others being hijacked by their analytical thoughts and work on your empathic skills. So, like Patrick and Kanthi, you can try to engage others in the possibility of moving beyond their first impressions. It's often what you put in that you get out, no matter how much diversity you try to bring.

- What is the first thing someone would notice about you when meeting you for the first time?
- How often do you take time to introduce yourself properly and engage with others before you share your thinking?
- What gets in the way of inclusion for you?
- What barriers do you see to inclusion at the company where you work?
- Are there some positive diversity, equity, and inclusion initiatives being implemented in your organisation?

Today's time-boxed online business world is itself a barrier to a fully inclusive workplace. It limits the opportunity to engage and reduces time for effective collaboration, planning and preparation. Collaboration allows leaders and others to feel supported as they work through the sometimes difficult challenges that stem from the need and desire to implement effective inclusive practices. Collaborative teams will help to identify best practices for inclusivity.

- What pressures on people are there outside the workplace?

Collaborating with others and being an empathetic leader will give you some insights into the experiences of others.

Patrick talks about a new role:

'Due to a job change, I needed to consider whether the post was right for me and whether I wanted to up sticks with my wife and leave everyone behind and relocate. I was discussing my dilemma with a close friend of mine, explaining that I had this great opportunity, that it was progression that I had joined the company for, and that my wife agreed with the move. My friend then stopped me and said, "Why do you want to move out there? There are no Black people out there. You don't belong there." There were no congratulations on the promotion, just a focus on "not belonging".

'I believed the fact that there would not be many Black people where we were going would not make any difference. Yet here was another black guy putting barriers up, talking negatively and suppressing what I saw as progression.

'It was like he was implying we should accept our status in life, that this is where we are at, we will always be oppressed, we must stick together as the people that feel sorry for ourselves and call out the establishment.

'In my view, I wanted to get involved to influence change and ultimately to build acceptance. I may not have thought about it consciously at the time. However, I knew that if I were going to progress and improve my ability to do good things with my life, I would have to change the way I went about it.'

The issues affecting progress for diversity, equity, and inclusion are systemic and behavioural. Once there is a clear understanding of these issues, then concrete strategies can be designed and implemented for real and lasting change. Continuous attention must also be paid to measuring success with its specific indicators and outcomes. Having a clear vision where a company wants to be with inclusivity over the next few years will help.

The role of a leader is to spell out that vision that presents a brighter tomorrow. It also needs an understanding of themselves as a role model of that vision, they must be connected to their vision and living it. The leadership team should have this shared vision for equality, inclusion, and diversity and engage with their wider teams to develop a shared understanding through dialogue, as well as enabling resources for skills development.

By collaboration and exploring partnerships throughout their organisations, they will also have clarity as to how individual and organisational relationships are formed, as well as how effective they are.

Skills development is key. There remains a gap between wanting to be inclusive and doing something about it. It is necessary to raise individual understanding of personal attitudes and beliefs, combined with an awareness of unconscious bias. Being willing to act will provide the boost to shift existing practices.

- What behaviours do you observe in this story?

Patrick's new role exemplified willingness to change. 'I became the senior manager of one of the inner-city factories. Demographics for the managerial and administrative roles did not mirror that of the surrounding urban conurbation.

'As I was given a tour around the factory, the demographics changed and reflected the ethnic mix of the surrounding areas more appropriately. There were lots of polite smiles and some looks of delight. This was from the black shop floor staff. I smiled back thinking nothing of it at the time.'

'I started to get my feet under the table and to get to know the people with whom I was working. Some of the black men started asking questions about pay and could I help them by paying a bit more. I asked what justification they had for this request and had they asked the previous manager.'

'The reply was no, but as one of us, surely you can do something to help us out. I responded by saying that you have no justification for being paid more than anyone else for doing the same job. It was like they wanted something for nothing in return, that I was obliged to do this because we shared the same colour skin and that out of loyalty to that I should risk my future by discriminating against others.'

Choice is the friend of inclusion. It is all about finding out what options people want and how they want to get involved. This is about identifying how individuals can participate. If you offer lot of options, then you are likely to get more diverse people involved in your activities.

In conclusion, be clear about your vision for equality, inclusion, and diversity and walk the talk. Make more time for your resources and allow for planning and collaboration. Be wary of your business systems, they are rarely conducive to positive change in the first instance. If business decisions are reinforced by compliance instead of quality engagement, you will not get buy-in or motivation from the people in the business. Be empathic with your colleagues. You do not know how difficult it might be for them to adapt to this different work environment, or what their peer pressure may be outside work. Finally, ensure that you have appropriate policies, tailored communications, and suitable behaviours to ensure you can reinforce the motivation. Let's examine the following scenario:

Patrick shares, 'I was on a factory tour with my line manager. It was the end of the working day and staff were waiting for the clocking out hour to arrive. Coming towards me on a bicycle in the factory was a member of staff. I stopped and explained that they should not be riding the bike in the factory and asked them to dismount. The staff member refused several times, so I directed them out of the factory.'

- As Patrick's line manager, what would you have said, how would you have supported Patrick in this scenario?

'The following day he came back to confront me. I knew that I had to deal with the situation in a way that would not compromise the organisation or me. I wanted to do the right thing and keep my credibility intact. I followed the laid-down policies and procedures.

'So, I absorbed the taunts by this former staff member as I led him through the office and out of the business: "Yeah, you Uncle Tom. You're not one of us, Uncle Tom."

'I was embarrassed at the taunts and angry also but knew I had done the right thing. I was not going to try and be a hybrid and have a foot in both camps. It just confirmed my decision to move on from the streets and leave those attitudes and behaviours behind.'

- Did the company policies and procedures support Patrick in carrying out his responsibilities or did they make a difficult situation worse?

Always consider your workforce's experience when working with your business. It's about the physical environment, of course, but it's the culture of the place they are in. We have discussed culture in a previous chapter. Make sure that everyone feels welcome both in the physical and non-physical environment. You can only encourage inclusion and diversity by expanding horizons.

There is no binary choice when it comes taking to the streets or following the establishment. We hope a well-orchestrated debate about the elements of diversity, equity, and inclusion can lead to wider understanding and increased opportunity. Debate is slow, yet it can help foster the conditions within which businesses can feel encouraged to move in a more inclusive direction and develop powerful motivating visions. Crucially, if more people are going to choose to leave the streets, this process must also seek to involve all stakeholders, including communities, political and religious leaders, and not forgetting the media.

- Does your personal vision for diversity, equity, and inclusion match your organisation's vision?
- What attitudes do you see in the business that support diversity, equity, and inclusion?
- What can you do differently to foster diversity, equity, and inclusion in your community?

CHAPTER 5

Speaking Up? Is It Worth Losing Your Job For?

'I was a recruit at my first company Christmas party,' Patrick Ricketts says. 'By this time, I had been to many other company Christmas gatherings and was no stranger to what happens when work colleagues are together, in a party setting, with free-flowing alcohol. Copious amounts of alcohol oils bravery and stupidity in equal measure and some people open their mouths before they put their brains in gear. The curious people. The obnoxious ones. The over-friendly types. This is where reputations can be destroyed or enhanced. It's certainly what everyone talks about in the weeks leading up to the next event. I knew I had to be on my guard, as always.

'On this occasion, one senior individual, who was drunk, made eye contact with me. He came over and started asking me questions. "Where are you from? You're not from around here? Do you work in the factory? I bet you can sing; I like to sing."

'I have been asked these sorts of questions a lot over time. They were all harmless, if a little irritating. I made my excuses and moved away from him.

'Later, the managing director asked me to help take the same person to a taxi, as he had become disruptive. Another colleague and I were taking him to the taxi when the drunken colleague punched me on the lip, causing blood to flow.

'How did it make me feel? For a split second, which seemed like ages, I wanted to knock him out! I remembered the questioning earlier that night, which, I felt, would not have been asked of someone that looked like him. I realised that is what would have been expected of my stereotype. Instead, I helped him into the taxi and went back into the party, trying to look like it had not affected me.

'To judge by the reaction of people on the night, I had behaved in the right manner. It brought me respect, support, and new friends amongst colleagues. The following week, the managing director came to see me and apologised again, not just for the punch but also for the questioning, which had been overheard. He said that the behaviour was unacceptable. The manager left the business soon afterwards. It became clear to me the managing director was sending a message to any others who thought that that sort of behaviour was acceptable in a business he was leading.'

- As a business leader, how would you have dealt with both these situations?

This chapter will consider when it is appropriate to stand up for personal values. When do you start to say, 'No, this is not acceptable behaviour,' and begin to stand up for what is right? When do you start to own the situation and take accountability for some of the outcomes? What are some of the changes needed in leadership teams and organisational cultures that will create a springboard for the shifts in behaviour necessary to give everyone the confidence to speak up and build accountability?

Inclusive leadership is about creating cultures where everyone feels psychologically safe and feels comfortable to speak up. That is a culture where everyone thrives. This book is about inclusive leadership when it comes to gender and ethnicity, yet it also has a much broader meaning. There are several aspects of diversity which we have no control over. These include gender, race, ethnicity, sexual orientation, physical ability, and even age. Other dimensions of diversity which we may have some control over include personal appearance, marital status, income, education, religion, work experience, personal values, political beliefs, and thinking style.

Dimensions of diversity

Things we have no control over	Things we have some control over
Age	Religion
Gender	Education
Physicality	Work experience
Race	Thinking style
Ethnicity	Personal values
Sexual orientation	Political beliefs
	Personal appearance
	Marital status
	Income

Many organisations today are building diversity, equity, and inclusion policies as part of their strategy. However, to truly change, it requires leaders to shift mind-set and create corporate cultures that are inclusive of everyone. Until then, even if organisations succeed in attracting people from diverse backgrounds, they will struggle with retention. These days, people do not tend to hang around if they feel they do not truly belong.

Inclusion is a combination of uniqueness and belonging. People who feel fully included feel understood and part of the group. They will believe they are psychologically safe and therefore empowered to speak up. There will also be people who are blending into the group to fit in but who do not feel that their identity is valued. This is referred to as assimilation or covering. I am sure we all know people who are adapting who they are to try to fit in, whether it is their style of clothes or personal background. Like sitting on a fence, this is an uncomfortable place to be in, and eventually can lead to dissonance. The opposite of inclusion or assimilation is that people feel their unique identity is recognised but that as individuals they are not accepted. The worst possible alternative would be that they feel excluded – that they do not belong or feel valued.

- What do you think was going on the following example from Kanthi?
- How inclusive was her client being?

'It was exciting,' Kanthi explains. 'I was working with a new client. My relationship seemed to be great, but my assumptions were based entirely on video calls. The journey to the manufacturing facility had been exhausting – two flights plus travelling for fifteen hours followed by a tiring, bumpy journey over poorly surfaced roads in the province.

'I presented myself to the board and shared my report with them. The company wanted to internationalise. I had suggested that culturally, the organisation was too stuck in its ways now. This did not go down well; however diplomatic I was being.

'Before I knew it, a wider meeting had been arranged in a location nearby and the hundred-strong senior management team assembled (they were all men bar two women) I wondered what I had walked into.

'Unfortunately, the client had taken my report personally and wanted support from his wider team. The content of the report was undermined by the group's desire to demonstrate respect for their seniors. Instead of accepting the feedback and remedies suggested in a positive manner, not intended to offend, they challenged the main observations from the report. They made it "wrong". Just before I left the meeting, I heard a couple of people put my approach down to my gender and ethnicity. It's a strange world. In the West, I am brown skinned. In the East, I am light skinned. Either place, I am still female.'

———— ✻ ————

Reinvention starts at the top of every organisation. As an inclusive leader, it is important to build empathy with your teams. It makes you more approachable while creating a psychologically safe environment for others. In turn, when people really start to believe that they can make a difference, they start to feel empowered and develop an attitude of personal accountability. This shifts the emphasis from 'keeping out of trouble' or 'keeping your head down' to acknowledging the reality and moving forward to an environment where everyone feels empowered and has the courage to speak up. We will see this later in the chapter when Patrick and Kanthi describe their experiences of challenging the status quo at senior level in their respective companies.

Being a fully inclusive leader needs multiple competencies, such as the ability to integrate diverse perspectives in a team by managing conflict while engaging a range of stakeholders. It also needs adaptability, courage, and the ability to build interpersonal trust while valuing differences. One of the first steps in this journey is to build empathy and to do this through building an understanding of yourself and a curiosity about others.

We would always ask leaders to look at themselves first and take ownership of their individual biases. As already alluded to, everyone has unconscious biases based on their own subjective experiences and dealing with these biases starts with the decision to do something about it. Once you have externalised these beliefs, recognise the red flags of your personal bias and rise above those thoughts and actions. So, avoid negative discussion of dissenting colleagues and try to see them as individuals. Remember: bias can lead to colleagues feeling powerless and can seed a culture of victimisation.

For instance, if a leader or team member refers to people of colour as a distinct group instead of seeing them as individuals, it can lead to unintended outcomes. Kanthi has a view on this: 'I refer to this behaviour as people as being "colour blind". I come across it frequently. It is especially noticeable where you can have a conversation with someone one day and the next day, they do not recognise you. When you say hello, they respond, "Oh, I didn't know it was you," with the implication that brown people all look the same to me.'

Kanthi changes the subject to describe a recent social situation prior to the Euro Football world cup in 2021. A group of people were discussing the final football match of the series between England and Italy. Kanthi, when asked, said that she was not going to watch the match. Someone from the group said, 'Well, I suppose you are not really English, so it's not so important to you.' When politely challenged, the response was that the assumption was skin-colour related.

- How would you have responded or reacted if you were Kanthi in a similar scenario?

The next day, England had reached their first final in a major tournament since winning the World Cup in 1966. It took place in Wembley Stadium, London, England, with thousands of fans attending and millions watching on television. Despite taking the lead against Italy,

England drew 1-1 after extra time before a penalty shootout. Three young black players missed penalties in the 3-2 shootout and were negatively targeted on social media after the game.

In the aftermath of the Wembley final, a row broke out over the UK government's handling of race and cultural issues as well as the lack of monitoring from social media platforms. At the start of the tournament, Johnson declined to condemn fans who booed England players 'taking the knee', the anti-racism gesture, while Home Secretary Priti Patel said fans had a right to boo.

'Taking the knee' became visible in sport during the national anthem played at an American NFL game in 2016. Quarterback Colin Kaepernick knelt on one knee to protest police brutality and racial inequality.

It became widely adopted in sport, and politicians, protesters, and police have taken a knee across the world to show their commitment to tackling racial inequality.

- What sort of biases did you observe in this description of the World Cup football match?
- What was the impact of bias here?

It can be intimidating to recognise one's own bias or to talk about what it feels like to be on the receiving end of it, but it's the only way to spark change. At the beginning of this chapter, Patrick described a situation where a colleague asked multiple questions about his ethnicity and threw in a few stereotypical questions, too. This is commonly referred to as microaggression. It is when a term is used, intentionally or otherwise, that communicates derogatory or negative attitudes. Over time, this can become a big deal to individuals who are regularly subjected to them. For example, Kanthi (pronounced *Karnthi*, for all sorts of reasons), started using one of her other names, Ella, as in the Western world her name was often mispronounced. She was called everything from Kay to Chianti and anything in between.

'When I hear two people call me Kanti,' she explains, 'and another two people call me Zante and someone else call me Shanti at the same time, I feel disaffected because I am needing more of a respectful attention as to my real name.'

- So as an inclusive leader, what would you do if you observed a colleague making a stereotypical comment that could be construed as microaggression?

So, what are the basic elements for human interactions in potentially challenging situations? They can all take place in the flash of an eye. First observe what is really happening in a situation, what are the others saying or doing to make the intervention more concrete. Consider your feelings when you observe this interaction? Offended? Scared? Amused? Irritated and so on? Finally, you must understand your needs connected to those feelings. Either way, it is important to make clear what is required from the other person. It is then up to them whether they will accept, reject, or make an alternative offer.

Observations are a crucial element of leadership. If we wish to be authentic and clearly and honestly express our views to another person from someone else's perspective is this what you want to say, or do you mean 'to a person who has a different perspective', then it is important to be clear as to what we are observing and with what context. For most of us, the ability to observe without making evaluations is difficult – labelling is habitual. When you are making observations of people and their behaviour try to remain free from judgement, criticism, and other forms of analysis.

The trick is to be able to articulate this observation without introducing any judgement or evaluation – to simply identify what we are observing that we either like or do not like. Then we explain what we have observed without causing offence or defensiveness. Finally, we could make a specific request. For instance, Kanthi could ask, 'Would you be willing to try pronouncing my name correctly, or would you rather use Ella?'

There are several other actions that can happen immediately when you observe a microaggression. You could change the topic or interrupt. You could use body language to show disapproval like frowning or getting up and leaving. Finally, as described above, you could talk privately to the person in question.

Eliminating bias means deciding to speak up when witnessing bias in others. Kanthi concludes, 'Speak out in that moment – that's how we can create a culture that doesn't tolerate this. Saying something as easy as 'that statement makes me uncomfortable' can send a message.'

In that context, it is interesting to share the post written by a colleague, Pratik Dattani, managing director of EPG, who is based in London, England:

'A conversation with a senior diplomat in London on a topic I've been thinking about for a few weeks motivated me to finally write this post. When three black players in the English football team were subjected to racist abuse after Euro 2020, it drew wide condemnation from their team-mates, royalty, politicians, and the country. It chimes with my general view that Britain is one of the most open, liberal, and fair societies in the world. It's a privilege for me to live here. The national reaction to Rashford, Sancho and Saka's treatment first nudged me to consider writing this:

> For the first time in many years, I experienced racism from a client recently. It so took me by surprise, I'm compelled to write about it. It wasn't the visceral kind the English players faced, but instead the passive-aggressive kind that says, "I'm better than you, because I'm white and you're not. I'm going to tell you what to do and how because, well, I'm white and you speak funny."

'It happened on successive video calls with three of my colleagues, two of whom are African, and one is half-African and half-Indian. I experienced it in calls I had with the person too, a condescension that comes from white privilege. I was shocked at his reaction when I mentioned the deaths of colleagues and family members during India's Second Wave of COVID just the week before. Clearly, a few fewer brown people in the world were not really something to concern oneself with.

'A colleague commented in private that this individual would try and arbitrarily change requirements (to the detriment of his employer) and sabotage a time-critical project we were working on, just because he didn't like us. I thought her concerns were overblown. But a few days later, that is exactly what happened. I escalated my concerns to the CEO, a black man, whose response was to ignore the racism, end the engagement midway and not pay invoices.

'To be clear: I'm not trying to be woke and jump on a cancel culture bandwagon. I understand that generations before me have suffered far worse. I'm grateful to them for paving the way for me to be able to call out this racism in a corner of Little England so easily today. But I've reached a level of seniority in my career that enables me to choose who I work with. And I choose not to work for racists, or those who enable racists.'

- As a leader how would you react if you heard a team member say they were feeling uncomfortable?
- Are you going to support it? How will you carry the whole team with you?

Empathising with people, understanding other points of view, is one of the powerful tools a leader has in their armoury. When someone really hears you instead of passing judgement or giving advice, it feels genuine. Sometimes, when things seem so complicated, just having someone listen without evaluation creates courage and strength.

Of course, it is much easier to empathise with a limited number of people, immediate peers, and other colleagues. Working in large organisations, many of which are hierarchical, there is a tendency to hear commands and judgement from the faceless seniors in the business. On the other hand, at board level, there is a predisposition to hear criticism and judgement from employees. As a leader, making the shift to look at the bigger picture, you might be tempted to overlook the situation. However, it is essential to consider the hints you may have missed and extra steps you could have taken. Consider also whether you are avoiding any risks. What or who did you fail to confront sooner? How did you make the situation worse?

Patrick became very aware that to be an inclusive leader means building empathy with your teams and looking out for your colleagues. He elaborates:

'The danger in business is that it can become less about the employees and more about delivering on KPI's for the company. Top performance can become all-consuming and on one occasion the company was proposing to cross the line of what I thought was acceptable.

'A business case was being presented at the board. It was for "zero hours" contracts for new starters in shop floor positions. Whilst from a financial point of view this made sense, the challenge for me was about having people working alongside each other, doing the same work but on different contracts of employment. In my view, it would be a ticking bomb. Even more, it contradicted the company vision and values and might potentially damage its reputation.

'I knew that people were already struggling to make a living on contracts that did not guarantee any regular work. In addition, most people coming into these roles were from local ethnic-minority groups. I made my case strongly to the board. I explained that it went against everything the company stood for as well as my values. Instead of treating people with respect the company was trying to take advantage of their desperation for work.

'I had worked side by side with these people on the shop floor. Some of the people that would be working on the new terms would probably be related. I knew that they had to take work as they could get it. For some of the people around the board table, they had never experienced this desperation and were unaware of the impact of their decisions.

'We needed to find an alternative way of making the numbers work. I stated that I wanted our company to become one of the top 100 UK companies and that this proposal would not help that ambition. Some board members looked at me in silence, others just bowed their heads over their papers.

'Eventually, the plan to change to contracts was shelved. It was progress of sorts, not the sea change needed. I still felt alone. There was silence after the meeting, but I got what I wanted and felt a sense of pride.

'Afterwards, I continued to build the courage to speak more freely about what the business should represent – diversity of thought, lived experience, gender, and race equality. I began recruiting women into senior managerial roles. I became active in recruiting management trainees from diverse backgrounds. This added richness to the business too, and showed what was possible outside of the board's original comfort zone.'

- Do you know and understand the demographics of the communities in the locations of your offices?

Patrick was demonstrating a sense of accountability and individual purpose by signposting a future that helped the boards face up to different realities and accept change. Leaders can encourage this sense of accountability and individual purpose which can build trust, develop positive employee experience, and raise engagement. This will increase psychological safety with those positive factors that lead to improved feelings of wellbeing. To generate a high sense of accountability it is important to understand that everyone has choices. When faced with a certain outcome, individuals can choose how to react it to it, also their long-term response and what else they can do to take things forward. As a leader, it is about looking beyond your individual tasks and responsibilities to the wider team.

Once you have created psychological safety within your teams, they will also feel empowered to make a difference. By truly giving responsibility to your team members, it will enable them to have responsibility to do the right thing. By involving people more in the way things are done, they will feel more committed to the business and work more effectively. To be most effective, empowerment must be rooted in the belief that everyone is important and can make a difference if this is acknowledged. If leaders are willing to devolve their power to everyone, they will provide the most fertile environment for everyone to contribute positively.

Empowerment can be a scary concept for many company leaders. It can be perceived as a loss of control and with that come trust issues.

- In the article below, Kanthi was behaving in an empowered way, what other behaviours do you observe?

'Recently appointed,' Kanthi says, 'I was producing a large company event to launch the company's new strategic direction and aspirations for wider inclusion. The three-day session required significant orchestration, with plenty of moving parts, multiple egos, and an internal political agenda of which I was completely unaware. The night before the keynote presentation by the CEO, he arrived to rehearse and make last minute amendments. It all went smoothly; however, he wanted one or two last minute changes. He announced that he was off home while that work was being done, which could then be sent on to him.'

'I suggested that as inclusion was one of his messages, he might be losing an influencing opportunity if he did not join his top senior people, five hundred of whom were in the room next door having dinner and staying overnight in the hotel. As I spoke, I noticed everyone melting away from around us, but I assumed it was to allow a more private dialogue. He did stay and everything went extremely well.'

'On Monday morning, my manager was summoned up to the CEO's office. Unbeknown to me, the CEO was quite volatile and had a notorious temper. When everyone moved away from us on Friday night, it was because they expected the CEO to explode and sack me for insubordination. Instead, he had called my boss to pass on a commendation to me for my courage in speaking up and prompting him back to his duties.'

'In some ways, it was a fuss about nothing. My job was to create an environment where people would be motivated to lead a new, dynamic, and inclusive culture. Ensuring the CEO was integral to that initiative was a part of doing my job. Would I have been so bold had I known he had a history of sacking people on the spot? I would like to think so.'

'However, in future I resolved that I would check the situation out and understand some of the key influencing behaviours as well as the dynamics of company politics before I jumped in with both feet.'

- What leadership behaviours do you notice in this story?

In earlier chapters, we discussed the importance of organisations being clear about their vision and values. In addition, leaders (at any level) need to understand how their personal values sit in the context of their company values. If the two do not coincide, it will end in multiple agendas running in tandem, at worst, or dis-engagement at best. It will certainly lead to inauthenticity across the management team. Without consistency between both business and personal values, there will always be disharmony with multiple splinter groups functioning at cross purposes across a business.

Patrick describes a disconnect in values for a company he was working for: 'The senior leadership team (SLT) recognised the business needed a big cultural change. They decided to arrange workshops for the regional teams. This included the regional team leaders attending the sessions with their direct reports.

'The content and delivery were different but effective. I did wonder whether the SLT had undergone the same training. If not, were they just ticking boxes? There seemed be a lot of 'do what I say, not what I do' behaviour going on.

'The managing director (MD) of the company attended one of the sessions and got involved in some of the post-breakout discussions. During one of these sessions, I questioned the company's customer-centricity at the regional level. Although it was acknowledged as a fair point by the MD, from the looks I was getting from others in the room, I could see I was stepping out of line. I believed it was important to share my views without fear of recrimination.

'Towards the end of the afternoon, there was a facilitated round table question and answer session. It included the MD sharing his personal journey to the top: what drives him, the hours he worked and how he got a lot from impromptu visits to parts of the business. The conversation turned to the detrimental impact on his personal life, on his children as well as his relationship with them. This was brushed aside, and the delegates turned back to focus on work.

'I was concerned by the implicit lack of importance attached to family and work-life balance, which is essential for everyone regardless of where you are in the hierarchy. His stories were macho stories and did not reflect the workshop emphasis on physical and mental wellbeing at work and home.

'When we reached the time for questions, I made the point that we all, regardless of role, need to think about work-life balance and the impact that will have on our children as they get older. It's all very well having our shoulder to the wheel all the time; however, it is important to have quality in our personal life. Success should not be at the cost of having no one to share it or not having a relationship with our kids as they get older or being part of a wider social group. Some of my peers and senior leaders were wincing at what I was saying. I thought the MD needed to consider that his example was the opposite of what we were advocating as the way forward.

'In the evening, some colleagues told me I would be toast. Others said that was a brave thing to do. For me, it was important to point out the inauthenticity of the SLT approach regardless of the personal consequences. There were others in the company more vulnerable than me that needed role models to follow. I wanted to work in a company that would do things differently, that would like to get the right balance between all the different things we do at work and life outside of work.

'Leaders and companies need to think about their impact on others when they make a point, whatever background they are from. It is also important to make others feel safe and supported in raising their own opinions. Providing open opportunities for people to talk without fear of negative repercussions can be important.'

- Do you believe that Patrick was correct in his approach?
- If you had been the MD, how would you have handled his questioning?

Amidst a global pandemic and heightened racial tensions, the importance of focusing on diversity, equity, and inclusion in the workplace and communities will rise to the front of many agendas. A truly inclusive company will prioritise areas such as gender, LGBTQIA+, and ethnic-racial diversity, enabling those with disabilities and encouraging local talent. Its leaders will understand that to leverage the human potential that exists within their business requires the establishment of relationships based on respect, listening, formal inclusion and zero tolerance for discrimination and harassment. These elements are all essential in building psychologically healthy environments. So, is speaking up worth losing your job for? In today's world, if you speak up and lose your job, then maybe you are in the wrong company.

CHAPTER 6

Making Relationships Work

The meeting was overrunning. Completing the agenda seemed like a long time away. Everyone was struggling to decide on a company change except Ashish. He was used to being in charge and expected everyone to just fall in with him. Mari-anne voiced a concern: 'I don't have enough information on which to base the decision. Besides, here in Sweden, we are used to getting consensus.' Meantime, BJ kept talking about the exciting things that would happen in the future. Leila wanted to please everyone and was feeling conflicted. Ashish started getting irritated with the impasse.
– Kanthi Ford

Diversity in the workplace encompasses far more than ethnicity or gender. Like an iceberg, it has hidden depths and encompasses more aspects than most people realise. So, diversity refers to visible and invisible aspects of identity that result in different work styles, problem-solving techniques, life experiences and perspectives. Some things you can see, some things may not be visible. The list is vast: age, race, ethnicity, socioeconomic class, parental or family or parental status, relationships, life experiences, neurodiversity, education, gender identity, disability, appearance and so on.

The differences in how people act and respond to the world around them, all contribute to the complex business world that leaders find themselves working in. Understanding how to lead diverse colleagues is essential in creating psychological safety, building trust, and driving innovation and performance excellence. Today's leaders must focus on motivating and inspiring others, not on directing them. Understanding themselves and their own biases is a critical skill.

Our history, values, beliefs, and interests shape our views of the world and filter the way we see things. Are you aware of the chewing gum analogy? Unfortunately, chewing gum has become the curse of modern town centres. It marks the sidewalks and pavements and costs a fortune to remove. Next time you are out and about in a city centre, look underfoot. I bet, once you have spotted these marks, you will keep seeing them. However, in the meantime, you have tuned out and selectively managed not to notice the marks.

If everyone sees the world differently, to grow as an inclusive leader it is important to try and look at the world from other people's points of view. This means being able to enhance both our internal and our external self-awareness. Internal self-awareness is how clearly, we see our own values, passions, aspirations, thoughts, and feelings. External self-awareness is understanding our effect on others and indeed, the effects of others on us.

The difficulty that most leaders have is that they are often unaware of the influence they have in an organisation. They may even be unconscious of the beliefs, behaviours, and attitudes they project. This leads to leaders frequently underestimating the impact of their behaviour on an entire organisation and often addressing the wrong issues when problems arise. However, while several traits are important for inclusive leadership, a leader's awareness of their own personal or organisation biases is the number factor that raters care most about (https://hbr.org/2020/03/the-key-to-inclusive-leadership). That is what was revealed by a Harvard Business Review analysis of 360-degree inclusive leadership assessments of more than four hundred leaders made by around four thousand raters.

Patrick shares his story:

'I had just been promoted as director for several business units up and down the country. Over several years, I had worked hard and delivered in every position that I had taken on, so I was delighted to have been recognised in this way. Most of the team that would be reporting to me had been peers for many years, and we had built up mutual respect.

'As I did my rounds in the first month in my new position, everyone was welcoming and congratulatory. I made the effort to let them know that I understood the challenges. I also knew the do's and don'ts to motivate my previous peers – especially not to come across as the big "I am". In the UK, this is a derogative expression to describe someone behaving as if they thought that they were the most important person in the world.

'One of my final visits was to a business unit I knew well; however, I did not know the manager. I was left waiting in reception for a short while and then taken to the manager's office where I introduced myself.

'It was not the first time that we had met but it felt like it. We shook hands but there was no warmth or eye contact from the manager. So, I set out what I had come to do, meet the team, tour the business unit, and have a one-to-one with the manager.

'In this session, the manager started to talk about why they were unhappy about not having a say as to who their line manager would be and how he did not see how my appointment would work. The manager went on to say that they did not like my style, could not see how I was going to help them and finally, that they were going to complain about it.

'I did my best to reassure the manager that whatever their concerns were that I was happy to listen to them and for us to work our way through them. However, who their line manager was would not change. No clarity was ever offered to me by the manager as to why they wanted someone else to be their line manager.

'Although my colour as an issue was not my first thought, later when discussing this reaction with someone who knew the manager well, I realised that this may indeed have been the issue. I had worked hard on building trust and thought I had built a good professional relationship. However, he now saw me in authority and felt challenged. This manager was only used to white middle-aged line managers, and I was not and looked different.

'It made me feel insecure. I started questioning how genuine my relationships were. It felt like, here we go again. I had the skills and experience and was the one who had to make the effort to show empathy and tread carefully, so there was no excuse that would justify any objections to me in whatever leadership role I had.

'After that, I tended to look purely on developing professional rather than personal relationships with colleagues because it was difficult to know where you stood with them.

'There were times when I was aware that I seemed a little standoffish. However, I was protecting myself from showing parts of myself because it might have been misread.'

- What effect did the interaction with his direct report (he does use the word manager) have on Patrick?
- What sort of behaviours was Patrick projecting in his response to the situation? Were they appropriate? What would you have done differently?

Did you know that direct reports and the wider group of employees tend to model their behaviours on their managers? This puts even more of a spotlight on the leader, not the employee. So, one of the keys to being an influential, inclusive leader is to understand how you impact others. Being clear on personal impact helps to distinguish managers and leaders. Managers tend to drive people for results. Leaders will be out at the front, shining a light on the path ahead and motivating people into action. Patrick talks about a relationship with a line manager:

'In my twenties, I accepted the role as a management trainee. Eventually, I got my chance to be a manager. This was in a rural town where you rarely saw another ethnic-minority person in the town or wider area that we served. I was the only Black person in the factory. I stood out visually.

'My industry experience and skills were not the issue. However, my management style was very different. Supervisors and line managers did not want to accept direction from me. Initially, my line manager, who did not want any confrontation with people he had worked with well for years, would try to coax me into accepting the old way of working, where everything was done for employees, and no one was expected to take accountability.

'He called me to the office and passed me a caricature of me sitting with my feet up at my desk. My manager said, "That's what they think of you."

'When I asked if he agreed, he prevaricated. However, he knew that I had been selected for this role to take the business forward. We understood that there were some cultural challenges on both sides and that I needed to meet them halfway. He did acknowledge the challenges of bringing in change for someone that looked like me and suggested I change some of my approaches whilst encouraging my peers and direct reports to change their behaviours. It all started to click. In the background, my line manager would be talking to my peer group and my direct reports explaining the changes and why.

'Back in those days, there was a lot of smoking and designated smoke breaks. This meant that to keep productivity at an acceptable level, substitutes from other production departments would step in to keep the flow going. There were also further breaks to fetch the ingredients to make sandwiches for the team.

'I had already calculated the annual cost and productivity improvement if we did things differently and had presented this to the management team at one of our many smoke-filled management meetings. As you can imagine, there was no appetite to support this as it would impact them and their teams.

'The supervisor had been working at the factory from her school days. She was in her fifties and incredibly influential with the shop floor and my line manager. I worked within the boundaries of what I could do and explained to the supervisor that some of the activity needed to stop because it was excessive. She chose to ignore my instruction.

'Although this issue was escalated and was supported at senior level, it was a real turning point in my career. At last, I had a line manager who understood me and believed in me, even though he found it difficult. I felt that he understood the challenges I faced and was now acting as my mentor.

'My confidence grew, and I learnt some important lessons that I would take with me as my career progressed. He made a lasting impression on me. Later in my career, he was more explicit about the challenges he recognised I faced and how proud he was of how well I had navigated those challenges because of the colour of my skin. We remained close right up to his passing early in 2021.'

There has been a great deal of research into the traits of successful leaders and into truly inclusive leaders. However, one aspect emerges ahead of the field – understanding yourself as well as others. In a Deloitte study, 'How Can You Show Up as an Inclusive Leader?' six signature traits of inclusive leadership were defined as important because they enable leaders to operate more effectively within diverse markets, make better connections with diverse customers, access a wider spectrum of ideas, and support diverse individuals in the workforce to reach their full potential. The six signature traits were defined as follows (https://www2.deloitte.com/insights/us/en/topics/talent/six-signature-traits-of-inclusive-leadership.html):

1. Cognisance – Are you mindful of your personal and organizational blind spots, and self-regulate to help ensure 'fair play'?
2. Courage – Do you speak up and challenge the status quo, and are you humble about their strengths and weaknesses?
3. Commitment – Are you committed to diversity and inclusion because these objectives align with your personal values and because you believe in the business case?
4. Curiosity – Do you have an open mind-set, a desire to understand how others view and experience the world, and a tolerance for ambiguity?
5. Cultural Intelligence – Are you confident and effective in cross-cultural_interactions?
6. Collaboration – Do you empower individuals as well as create and leverage the thinking of diverse groups?

As we have said repeatedly, everyone has their own personal biases. Our individual experiences, values, beliefs, and interests shape our personal filters and the way we look at the world. Problems arise when you assume that everyone sees the world the same way as you do. If their style is different, then it can lead to misunderstanding and consequent alienation of team members. Patrick shares an example:

'I had worked on and off with my colleague for over twenty years since I was a management trainee. During that time, I went from being a wet behind the ear newbie to a board member. We had a mutual respect and were good friends outside of work.

'I was aware of my colleague's approach to getting things done, which sometimes clashed with my approach as well as that of others. There was a board reshuffle, and my colleague had to report directly to me. I was apprehensive, I knew that there would be a clash of styles at some point, and I wanted to nip it in the bud. My colleague liked to work from instinct and did not always clearly think through solutions. I liked to have data, empirical evidence to reach sustainable solutions. I met with my colleague off-site to explain this issue and to agree on a way of working, going forward. We realised that the dynamics had changed, in the early days I was always willing to learn, and my colleague was glad to oblige. We shared similar values in terms of wanting to get things done, although we had different ways of getting there.

'He agreed that we would work on our weaknesses and use our strengths to take the business forward. We became more open about what views we had on projects and issues. Rather than keeping them to ourselves we shared our perspectives and came to a consensus which made us more effective as a team and this led to success in our areas of responsibility. Our working relationship flourished once more, and we remain close friends to this day.'

How do you figure out someone else's style?

There have been centuries of research into the way we are wired as humans. From the archetypes of Plato through to Kant, Jung, Freud, and so on. Greek philosopher Plato and Swiss psychiatrist Jung both spoke about how archetypes influence and define who we are through behaviour. Plato believed archetypes to be mental forms embedded in the soul prior to birth. Jung identified archetypes as elements of the 'collective unconscious' that can be identified through behaviour. According to Jung, archetypes are the foundation of our personality, drive, feelings drive, beliefs, and actions.

Over decades, organisations have produced in-depth information about archetypes and, indeed, many personal evaluations and psychometric evaluations derive from them. Understanding something about core archetypes and especially your personal archetypes can help you develop insights into what drives you and makes you tick. There are numerous populist evaluations such as DISC and Insights profiles which can help you on the journey. However, this is not the book for us to go further into detail on this subject, any internet or library search on the subject will provide you with a wealth of information.

If you understand the theory of archetypes and what they tell us about ourselves and others, you can use that information to do two things: the first is to understand yourself better. So, by knowing more about your core temperament, you can leverage your strengths and adapt your weaknesses to improve your outcomes as a leader. The second opportunity comes from identifying how others show up based on observation. Putting this knowledge together with knowledge of yourself, can really improve your management approach and customise each interaction. Here is a broad approach to four different types:

Type	Extrovert Thoughtful	Extrovert Emotional	Introvert Emotional	Introvert Thoughtful
Personality Preference	Direct No emotion	Direct Feelings clear	Indirect Emotional	Indirect Non-emotional
Appears	Business-formal	Stylish	Casual	Conservative
Work Preferences	Active Formal Efficient Structured	Stimulating Personal Cluttered Friendly	Personal Relaxed Friendly Informal	Structured Organised Detailed Formal
Style	Decisive	Spontaneous	Easy-going	Systematic
Focus	Task oriented	Relationships	Support	The process
Fears	Loss of control	Loss of prestige	Confrontation	Embarrassment
Under tension will	Be assertive	Challenge	Acquiesce	Avoid
Likes	Results	Recognition	Attention	Accuracy
Is concerned with	Why? What? When?	Value Impression Uniqueness	How it will affect them personally	The logic The purpose
Seeks security in	Control	Flexibility	Relationships	Preparation
Wants to maintain	Success	Status	Relationships	Credibility
Supports their	Objectives	Relationship	Warmth	Analysis
Seeks to achieve acceptance by	Competing	Playfulness	Conforming	Thoroughness
Likes you to be	Brief	Outgoing	Pleasant	Precise
Wants to be	In control	Admired	Liked	Correct
Is irritated by	Indecision	Routine	Insensitivity	Unpredictability
Measures personal worth by	Track record	Compliments	Compatibility	Precision
Decisions are	Quick	Spontaneous	Thoughtful	Slow

Consider these rule-of-thumb assessments that are based on four main traits or profiles:

- What behavioural type best describes you?

- What strengths have you identified?
- What would you perceive as your challenges?
- Do you have a specific type or person with whom you have more in common?

Kanthi shared the time when she met someone who was to become a long-term colleague in her consulting business. 'When we first met, MC had no time for me. I admired his attention to detail and cautiousness whereas he felt challenged by my big picture approach. This led to him initially avoiding working with me. Eventually, through running several client sessions on personality styles, we came to understand both our strengths and weaknesses. We even began to use ourselves as examples of style with our workshop delegates.'

These general assessments are based on four main trait or profile types. As described in the tables above, these are based on thinking extroverts, thinking introverts, feeling extroverts, and feeling introverts. They can help us to gain insights into our teams and our peers as well as more self-awareness. In turn, as business leaders, this also helps us to assist in empowerment, motivation, and action. So, by using these tools, we hope it will help you to better understand yourself and others and improve your communication with peers. It can also assist you with a non-judgmental framework to discuss issues in a non-confrontational way.

Patrick shares an example: 'A colleague took a genuine interest in my career and life experiences and because I was now much more experienced and comfortable in my skin, I started to share, as I found him to be good company and someone that trusted. He was an introverted person whereas I was more of an *extrovert*.

We felt that we had things we could learn from each other and were able to challenge each other safely. He considered me as someone that could role model for others. My style had influenced his thinking, and he used this insight to ensure his decision-making considered all the areas it should. We understood how we could benefit from each other and were both receptive to challenges, change, and ideas.'

Confrontation can happen if we are unable to understand or appreciate other people's points of view and how we/they react to different situations.

By gaining an insight into someone else's style, you can accommodate it and adapt to it to improve interactions.

Here are some areas of conflict that can occur in a business context:

Type	Extrovert Thoughtful	Extrovert Feeling	Introvert Feeling	Introvert Thinking
Tipping point	Frustrated by lack of urgency in others. Irritated by emotions and feelings	Frustrated by indecision and extensive detail.	Uncomfortable around assertive people and conflict	Frustrated by lack of detail and others' emotional response
Way forward	Relate to your own feelings. Empathise with others	Slow down. Recognise some people need to dwell in the data to make decisions.	Understand the need to deliver results. Stop taking conflict personally	Learn how to limit analysing everything and be more enthusiastic.

- What issues do you see in this discussion below with Patrick?
- With this knowledge of different personal styles, what could have been done differently?

Patrick Ricketts speculates, 'How do you get on and interact well with your colleagues to make the job more enjoyable? How can you build trust and mutual respect, and support each other? I have found there are red lines that some colleagues won't cross when they see how you are treated differently by your other white middle-aged colleagues. Why is that? Why was I always the one having to go the extra mile to make the relationships work? In more recent times, I have found this less of an issue so how much has the situation improved over time?

'Let me give you an example of a customer meeting. I have found that in front of customers, the struggle to prove that you belong and are worthy of holding a senior role has been challenging over the years. I have lost count of the number of times that I have been asked for my credentials.

'I was due to make my first visit to a large national customer with one of my team. I had been fully briefed on what we were there for, and I had the names of all the customer attendees. We were led into a large conference room and were joined by five people – the national buyer, their assistant, and three department heads.

'The buyer was leading the meeting. He introduced his colleagues and said why they were there. My colleague was the account manager, so no introductions needed there. I introduced myself, and then the questions came – "Oh, how long have you been in the business? When did you get this role? What have you done before this? What is the organisational structure?"

'After the meeting, my colleague said to me, "I don't know what got into him. He's not usually like that."

'I said, "I reckon he is not used to seeing people like me representing large organisations at my level." On reflection, and now living in different times, I would spend more time explaining to my colleague what was happening to accelerate understanding.

'From that point on, I was always ready to do my pitch as if I was on autopilot, even when I was not asked, which, in hindsight, was wrong. I should not have felt the need to justify why I was there and what I could do for them. It was demeaning and exhausting.

'Eventually, though, what was more important? The customers' curiosity and retaining them, or my self-respect, so I stopped answering every question. I would ask why it was important to know that.

'I did work hard at that meeting to prove to them that I knew what I was doing and that I had earned the right to be in the room. Eventually, the buyer and I struck up a good working relationship that lasted a long time. He valued my perspective on situations and challenges and respected the innovative solutions I brought to the table.

'How did it make me feel? I had to prove that I had the right to be there and give a précis of my journey before they would take me seriously and trust me. I had to share my journey just to satisfy their curiosity. I didn't share this with anyone, and I did not believe that they would understand. I thought that they would just brush it off as me being oversensitive. You develop an instinctive radar for a line of questioning.'

- If you were the leader in that meeting, would you have had the same questions?
- What would you do differently and why?

- If you were Patrick's line manager, how aware would you have been of the issues he would be facing? How would you have checked if he was OK?

Microaggressions

We have discussed unconscious bias however the term *microaggression* is being used more frequently. A chapter about building effective relationships would not be complete without a short discussion to raise your awareness about microaggressions. So, what are they? The everyday (often unintended) demeaning messages, insults as well as derogatory or negative attitudes conveyed by people who are frequently well-intentioned but unaware that they are in a dominant group. Microaggressions are often discussed in a racial context but anyone in a marginalised group such as gender, sexual orientation, disability, or religion can experience one. So, how can that be seen in the workplace?

Kanthi takes up the story: 'A microaggression I regularly come across is the "Where do you come from?" question. For instance, recently, I was working in the north of England, and this pleasant gentleman I had just been introduced to at work asked me precisely this.

'First, I had to remind myself that he was being curious and was unaware that it was a microaggression to me. So, I took a deep breath and answered, "I was born in Surrey," and countered with, "Where do you come from?"

Fortunately, it deflected the situation, as quite often, people come back to me with, "Where are you really from?" They are tiny comments that reflect assumptions about people based on some aspect of their perceived identity. So, the speaker's bias shows up, and they may be unaware of it.'

Usually, we observe people looking quite confused when we raise this topic. They suggest they are being just being curious, for instance. Yes, innocuous comments may appear as compliments or genuinely expressed questions, but they could be unintentional expressions of racism, sexism, and other types of discrimination.

Just be aware that they are labelled microaggressions because they are small and because of their size, they are easy to miss. Here are a few examples of common racial microaggressions in the workplace starting with Kanthi's least favourite question.

Where Are You Really From?

Both Patrick, as a second-generation Jamaican, and Kanthi, as half Asian, have lost count of the times they have been asked this. This microaggression creates an 'othering 'effect. It sends a clear message that the recipient tis 'not one of us' or 'from around here.' Small comments that reinforce being outside the dominant group.

- Can I call you K for short? When someone mispronounces a peer's name or asks if they mind being called something else (because they are not willing to take the time to learn to pronounce a new name), it sends the message that the person of colour is different. It almost feels like name shaming. Most people are likely to say yes and become internally frustrated.
- Can I touch your hair? This is one of Patrick's bugbear microaggressions. It again reinforces that the person is different. It is an odd thing to request to touch anyone's hair.
- Would you mind organising teas and coffees, lunch, or taking the minutes? This used to be one of Kanthi's pet hates when she first started working in business. The assumption that the woman in the group will take on these roles by default is inappropriate.
- You speak such good English! At first this may sound complimentary. However, depending on the tone and context, it can come across as quite patronising, as if they didn't expect people of colour to have been so articulate.

It is all a bit of a minefield. Microaggressions will vary from person to person, depending on context and individual history. It is tempting to ignore microaggressions, but the build-up of these everyday slights can have consequences for a person's mental and physical health if overlooked. It is wise to understand more about microaggressions, but do not start to avoid people of colour in case you say the wrong thing! If you unintentionally offend someone, apologise, and learn from it. Always be authentic and open to learning. If you are unsure whether something may be offensive, speak up. People usually respond positively when asked. Remember: discrimination, however subtle, has consequences.

- Can you think of some examples of microaggressions?
- What would you do if you observed them at work

CHAPTER 7

Changing People's Views

Kanthi Ford says, 'I felt unique. There was nobody like me at pre-school, nursery or in my street. I was lucky. Later, at school I felt alienated. There was no one dark like me at the English schools. I fitted better in a Sri Lankan school, although I was too English there.

'In my teenage years, there was no actor, pop star, or anyone on my television screen like me. So, during my teenage years I withdrew from the world. Diversity comes in many guises. I know what it is like to feel excluded and apart. There is great power in realising you are not alone, that there are others like you. Feeling connected with others gives you the strength to be yourself and belong. The people and stories we hear and see on screen and in our daily lives play a big role in enabling that connection.'

As our readers will know, throughout this book, we have been describing our separate journeys through life and our experiences as people of colour in a business world. Kanthi Ford continues, 'The main thrust of this chapter has fundamentally changed following my recent business visit to another European country. I had believed that the overt racism, "being picked on", that I had experienced on occasions throughout my life was something of the past. Unfortunately, the arrival of the COVID-19 pandemic in 2020 with its resultant wave of fear combined with an anti-Asian sentiment, has activated racism at an unbelievable level.'

Kanthi continues, 'In December 2021, I travelled abroad to work with clients on a leadership session. Arriving in the busy immigration hall, as two planes must have arrived simultaneously, I was preceded by several hundred other people. I took to one of my favourite occupations – people watching. I noticed that there were multiple officials in a filtering role, checking arrivals' paperwork before they were passed through to the border officials. Two things occurred to me. First, one of these "filter guards" was quite aggressive towards people of colour. The second was that, once these people got to the border officials, they were taking twice as long to question them in contrast to their white counterparts. As I was queuing for well over an hour, this trend was consistent throughout that time.

'How naive I was. Somehow, I did not apply this newly found insight to myself! Unfortunately, I found myself facing the same "filtering" I had observed. I still assumed they would treat me differently and was incredibly wrong. The official was aggressive in the extreme, confiscated my passport, and made me stand aside. (Later I found out from her supervisor I had made her "very angry" as some of my documentation was on my phone and not printed out – not a requirement.) When I finally got to speak to the border official, he took half an hour to question me before stamping my passport and allowing me entry.

'So, what did I learn? That fear can change people's behaviours in any organisation. When added to the trappings of power – uniforms, bureaucracy, and so on – it can become skewed. Two years ago, March 2020, when I visited the same airport for a similar workshop, these attitudes and behaviours were not visible. This was just as the country was going into lockdown at the start of the COVID-19 pandemic and its consequent restrictions. At that time, Chinese restaurants were being targeted by protestors and had been forced to shut as they were being blamed for releasing the virus. Clearly, in Italy, the horrors of the pandemic, trucks loaded with COVID-19 victims, being driven through the streets combined with an extended lockdown have surfaced these racist undercurrents.

'Government propaganda enhanced by media hype also influences fear. I witnessed this in another European country in the same year, March 2020. The attitudes of the French to the English have been well documented. Many say that this was entrenched before Napoleonic times. Most of the time, the French tolerate the English. However, at the start of the pandemic, the French media was full of the news that COVID-19 was rife in the UK and it was infecting the French. I was staying at a French family hotel in early March. Reception was staffed by the charming elderly father of the owner. Or, at least, he was charming on Thursday. However, on Tuesday, the country went into lockdown. As I was leaving for the airport, I approached him to request a travel form that was needed to show to the gendarme. It was quite a shock when he backed away with his hands protectively raised in front of him, shouting in French, "Keep away! Keep away!" It took me back to my early career if I was out and about to meet with the public. People would often back away from me, muttering racist comments.'

So, how does it apply to you, our reader? Well, it certainly isn't going to change the views of any of those people, but it shows the importance of having the insights to understand our own biases as well as how they show up in our behaviours and beliefs. Self-knowledge is an essential ingredient for any person. You need to know yourself before you know others.

The events of the early 2020s – the COVID Pandemic, George Floyd's death and the rise of the Black Lives Matter and Me Too movements – have all accelerated awareness of 'difference' as well as minority groups and, the challenges they face socially and in the workplace. These events have been highly visual in the media, highlighting the issues and calling for the need to change. So, this penultimate chapter of our book must explore how diversity, equity, and inclusion can this be articulated in the workplace and how do leaders, whatever their home base, effectively lead the changes that need to happen for a more diverse, equitable, and inclusive approach.

So, what does a chairperson or CEO need today? Traditionally organisations are driven by shareholders and the need for profits, dividends, and growth. So, what behaviours and personal values will be required to attract, nurture, and retain diversity? How do people lead diversity, equity, and inclusion with their teams, whilst keeping the rest of the organisation on track? Will they be brave enough to rearrange their teams if they do not share those values? Are you mindful of your personal and organisational blind spots? Do you self-regulate to ensure fair play?

It must be recognised that we are all wired with our own biases. So, understanding this and then recognising them and where they occur is essential. In acknowledging how they affect you personally, it will help you to consider the bigger picture rather than your personal agenda. Building an understanding of the appropriate behaviours to underpin a truly diverse culture does not happen overnight. If you wish to include people from all walks of life and multiple generations being clear about the language that is commonly used is a big step.

Patrick Ricketts added, 'Being black and brought up through the 1960s and 1970s, there were expressions used then that have less of an impact on me than they would on young black adults now. Some denigratory expressions are no longer part of everyday parlance. I had become desensitised. As a youth, there was no way of challenging such language without reprisals or being marked out as difficult with a chip on your shoulder. It was a very difficult time with a lot of biting your tongue with pent-up frustration or anger that had to be kept under control publicly. In private, amongst peer groups we would safely let rip about what we all had to deal with. It was our therapy.

'In some companies that I have worked for, there were inner sanctums. I know what it felt like being part of the out-group and well as the in-group. I used those feelings and experiences to ensure that consideration is given to everyone I worked with. I made sure that they were encouraged to participate, that their thoughts and ideas were welcomed.

'In the earlier years of my career for this very reason, I chose not to rock the boat when I was being excluded because I knew that it would not help my career progression.'

It is challenging for those that have not experienced exclusion in any shape or form to understand the impact on those who have. People who have been born privileged can simply be unaware of background differences which means it will be difficult for them to have empathy. So, it is important that those groups with different experiences are not afraid to share. They should be able to express how being part of an out-group has made them who they are, how it makes them feel and its effect on them. Business leaders benefit from hearing individual and personal truths about the culture within their businesses. The current online environment makes it easier to share in real-time compared to the past when, by the time your message was shared, the originator could be seen as 'vocal' or as 'difficult' in an organisation.

Inappropriate behaviour should be addressed constructively in an evidence-based way to allow the leadership team to understand, have more empathy and alter their approach. Finally, it is essential to lead by example. For any change to become sustainable, leaders cannot delegate this as another initiative for the human resources department. Everyone needs to own it, change the status quo, and manage the changes.

Managing change of every kind is an essential part of leadership. A natural response to change is resistance. At its best, this can provide an opportunity to discuss and engage others. At its worst, it feels insurmountable. Right now, change is everywhere. People are struggling to understand what constitutes acceptable societal rules and interpersonal workplace behaviours. Most leaders, managers, supervisors, or team leaders underestimate the resistance to change that they will experience. They also fail to consider the time it will take to create the shift. However, resistance to change is as natural as change itself. So, leaders must learn how to anticipate and understand resistance as well as the barriers it creates.

Change is an emotional issue. As people face doubts, uncertainties, and fears, they experience self-doubt, the feel they are being pushed out of their comfort zone and into an unknown destination. So, in addition to leading the change, learning how to overcome resistance is equally important.

Encouraging people to consider the possibilities ahead, is one way to climb over any barriers. A constructive outlook allows people to see both the pluses and minuses around a situation. Organisations that encourage positive outlooks nourish new ideas and beliefs. In a flexible, open culture, employees feel free to share their thoughts and new ideas more readily.

Courage is essential for a leader. Do you speak up and challenge the status quo? Are you humble about your strengths and weaknesses? Progressive leaders will recognise their biases and shortcomings and are prepared to address them regardless of personal risk. They are happy to show their vulnerabilities because they want to be part of that change. They know change is coming and that it needs to happen. They will also be willing to challenge the status quo and explain the impact it has on others. In this way, more people can help bring about changes in behaviour.

Educate rather than create more alienation, combative or dismissive mind-sets. Be part of the solution by being articulate and measured in your reasoning to influence change in people. Although it may seem obvious, it's the how to bring about change that's the challenge.

So, the first step is to communicate the why. People need to understand why change is being made. People want to know that the result will justify the possible upheaval. Leaders need to demonstrate this by investing in people and actively working with their teams to build shared desire and understanding of why there must be change, working on how to make the changes, and sustainably embedding them.

Leaders must be mindful of what is said, and how their teams react to what is being said as well as how they interpret the way others speak and feel. Don't close people down. Treat everyone fairly. Encourage colleagues and you will gain more understanding which, in turn, will influence how you move forward more effectively.

Shift the bias you have from bottom-line results to creating an innovatory, learning culture that visibly embraces diversity, equity, and inclusion. Of course, you are likely to risk losing a high performer who no longer fits with the direction the company now wishes to take but the dividends will be worth it.

For leaders and people to stay on the path of diversity, equity, and inclusion while remaining authentic, there are bound to be bumps along the road to change.

Patrick continues his story:

'I had made it to the top table by overcoming all the challenges mentioned previously. Yet I was on the outside. Following a senior leadership meeting, I said to a peer that I felt there was an inner sanctum as decisions that I should have been part of were being delivered to me without consultations. There was in-group favouritism and that they preferred to work with group members that shared the same values. I was never sure whether this was a deliberate or a subconscious trait of the team however, it did leave me feeling isolated at times and knocked my confidence. This was met with a shrug of the shoulders and a comment that I was being paranoid. Being a black man in a white man's world I have now learned to behave differently?'

Getting the fundamentals right in the first place is key to shifting colleagues forward in a non-threatening nurturing way. First, we must all accept that bias is a cognitive issue. We are all wired for bias. Our lifetime experiences from birth will have created the complex labyrinth of beliefs and biases that drive our behaviours. Business leaders need to be aware of their own biases as well as those of their teams. It is important to be aware of how inaccurate assumptions can narrow perspective and drive inappropriate behaviours. They should figure out personal strategies to override those biases. These interventions will be vital in changing peoples' views and making positive progress with equity, diversity, and inclusion in their company. So, consider calling out inappropriate behaviours in real time and providing feedback to individuals on what they said or did and how it may have been perceived by others. Above all, be consistent in approach, clear in communication and be fair to everyone.

Unconscious bias is endemic in recruitment policies and processes. Patrick explains:

'In the companies that I have worked there were entrenched views on what the profile of senior managers and management trainees had to be. I decided to challenge these views and I was confronted with incredulity and bemusement. My sense was they did not want to make it difficult? In essence, why change what they have always done? Instead, play safe and recruit people who appear like us, recruit so that we don't have to make much of an effort in a way that appears less risky.'

'My view was that this does not drive change in a business and therefore I challenged recruiters to put candidates from diverse industries, genders, and backgrounds in front of us. We succeeded in recruiting talented candidates from minority groups and women into senior leadership and management trainee posts. Therefore, acknowledging what is needed now and preparing for the future leadership of the company by ensuring that their perspective is incorporated to ensure inclusivity for the future of the company.'

Curiosity can play a large part building the links between widely diverse groups in your organisation. Patrick explains his own experience:

'I have not always had an open mind-set as to how others see the business unit I was leading. I was not open to new ideas at all, I just wanted results. After all, this was how my bosses became successful. Eventually, this led to a team of people that just said yes to everything.

'I finally realised that this led to stagnation, a disengaged team, and a lack of innovation. It also caused huge frustration on my part. It forced me to reflect on what turned me off from my bosses, so I changed my approach.

'I decided to ask more questions of the teams I was working with. I really wanted to get their views so that I could learn from their experiences and include those in my thinking. This helped me to understand other points of view and get better engagement from everyone. People felt included in the decisions and direction of the business.

'A company I was working in had some complex challenges at one of its factories. I asked questions and actively listened to the senior leadership team, customers, frontline, and back-office employees.

'The richness of information that came from customers, frontline, and backroom employees was invaluable. This helped me obtain the perspectives I needed to help devise solutions to the challenges faced. All parties appreciated being included in the conversation, particularly the customers, frontline, and backroom employees.'

⎯⎯⎯⎯⎯⎯ ⦚⦚⦚⦚ ⎯⎯⎯⎯⎯⎯

One way to understand an organisation's attitude to change is to look at the how it responds to new ideas. Creating an environment where people feel free to generate and innovate is critical to business survival. Surprisingly few organisations actively encourage ideas sharing especially outside normally perceived boundaries. The freedom to try and embrace new ideas requires a psychologically safe environment. A workplace which empowers individuals will pay dividends.

- How will you leverage the thinking of the diverse groups in your business?

As the senior leader, never be afraid to ask about what you don't know. None of us have all the answers. Sometimes senior leadership teams can be wary of subjects outside of their comfort zone. This restricts their learning stifles the generation of new ideas and reduces engagement the opportunity to incorporate diverse perspectives in overcoming barriers to improving customer service and employee engagement.

Being inquisitive increases what we know and creates further questions from which new ideas are generated. Therefore, the more people you include you learn more which helps you identify your limitations, and your communication becomes more informed. Others start to feel more valued and therefore gain the confidence to contribute to the changes required. So, do you have an open mind-set combined with a desire to understand how others view and experience the world? Do you have a tolerance for ambiguity?

While a set of technical drawings or a process map can depict the performance of a system or piece of equipment in an organisation, the reality when it comes to culture is rarely so simple. All businesses have a subjective, or invisible side, which influences success or failure. The difference between success and failure is often ascribed to a limited set of shared values and organisational behaviours that combine to create a high-performing culture in which all employees are excited about their work and tend to be more involved in the business.

- What happens when you underpin organisational culture with national cultures?

Patrick takes up the story: 'As my career progressed my cultural references started to be influenced by my working environment. My thinking subconsciously shifted from Afro-Caribbean thinking and experiences to one that fitted more with my working environment where I was usually one of one. This was not my intention however, if you're in an environment long enough you will be influenced by it.

'This became a real struggle for me as I realised as I feared losing my identity. The people that I was socialising with, which was now by and large people connected to work. On the weekends I reconnected with my roots through playing sport and clubbing. In hindsight this kept me connected and grounded.

'In those earlier years, it was difficult to exhibit who you really were without being seen as having an issue with people in the workplace or socially as you were expected to behave because they evaluated other cultures according to their preconceptions originating in the standards of their own culture, usually that the other should default to a subservient role. Therefore, I assimilated to fit in. Did it hurt? Well, it all happened organically. Mostly, however, there were times when it was through gritted teeth. Disturbing when I reflect on it now.

'As time went on, I had this desire to be my authentic self, not to suppress who I was to keep the peace and leave others in their comfort zones. I wanted to express myself, share my views, add a different perspective and influence thinking and show I have more to offer than just doing the job. I started to share different cultural perspectives so that they could consider these in their day-to-day thinking. I wanted to be seen as a black man that could make it in the establishment by being my authentic self however, with an understanding of other cultures without being overly familiar with those cultures to the point of being laughable by overplaying what I knew and understood but enough to gain other cultures confidence and show that I appreciated their difference.

'This was even more evident in the lack of understanding of the Asian class system. In one of our most ethnically diverse factories with a team of white, Afro-Caribbean, eastern European, and Indian groups, a manager promoted an Asian lady into a supervisory role. The promotion was based on the core competencies she had demonstrated and her and her ability to lead a team. It soon became clear that this was not going to be a total success as one Asian lady refused to accept that her superior was from a lower caste. The supervisor was of the Vasikya caste, her surname was Bhalkat, which is one of the many surnames associated with Vaishya.'

'This was a challenging issue for the manager who was born and bred in the Shires and had no knowledge of this. He struggled to resolve the situation he found himself in. He could not reverse the decision to promote Mrs Bhalkat, nor could he ignore the fact that Mrs Kaur was refusing to take instruction from Mrs Bhalkat. No amount of arbitration seemed to work, and ultimately, the performance management process was used successfully to calm the waters.'

In many ways, the two ladies described were not assimilating the Western approach to performance management, and their manager was out of his depth. This will happen and should be positively acknowledged, rather than ignored. Today, this would have called for some intercultural awareness engagement and an open discussion between all three parties as to a reasonable way forward.

As a leader, it is vital to be authentic in your interactions. It is also important to be clear how your demeanour and behaviours will be perceived by those from different backgrounds so that you don't offend. Get an understanding of how ethnically diverse your organisation is and try to understand them culturally. Do you know and understand the demographics of your workforce. How much effort have you made to ensure you know and understand and that your leadership group do also?

Corporate culture provides the intrinsic meaning, direction, and clarity to mobilise the collective energy of people in the company. Underpinning this is a myriad of national and tribal, small group cultures, which combine to form the organisation. Rarely do a leader and their teams start off with or share the same values and perspectives. This sense of unease can be somewhat more challenging when people from diverse backgrounds are in the mix, whether they are employees, customers, or stakeholders.

So, in conclusion, leaders need to ensure that all voices are heard and have the confidence to ensure everyone feels valued, empowered, and able to contribute their individual perspectives. It also takes people from diverse backgrounds to step up and be brave in being their authentic selves at work and challenge behaviours that stifle inclusion. Successful leaders do not create a successful business on their own. They need to be great facilitators that can get the best out of their teams.

- How would you as leader create a safer environment for people to express their frustrations and how the culture of their working environment affects them?
- As a leader how would you ensure inclusion for all, would you be able to recognise if it were not happening?

Conclusion

This book is essentially a summary of our intent and request for you, our readers, to take the learning forward.

It is our attempt to provide insights into a few small aspects of the things that contribute to the umbrella title of 'Diversity, Equity, and Inclusion.' All cultures are different, but leadership is about understanding context, being clear about our personal biases and celebrating both similarity and difference. All aspects of cultural diversity intersect and there are multiple distinctions to be aware of. Diversity covers a huge list. From gender to age, ethnicity to religion or educational status.

Your commitment as a leader to developing our understanding to build collaborative cultures in the future will be essential. Like a musical composition, there are multiple layers to understand and develop. When well combined, the result will be music to your ears.

We would like this book to provoke business leaders into action and build their organisational cultures in a way that is sustainable and becomes business as usual.

What Are You Going to Do Differently?

Look at yourself first and recognise the impact that your personal belief systems and behaviours have in driving the culture in your teams and your businesses. Take some time to reflect. Find out more yourself and what you would like to change about yourself before you turn to your work and start the journey of change there.

Time? It is the one commodity that all leaders, wherever we speak to them in the world, claim to have little of. Yet, effective use of time is a simple process. Just book a fixed time slot in every day to decide what is important to you and what is not. Then marginalise activities which are not important to you.

So why do we get bogged down in everyday things? Think about the number of things you do that don't get you anywhere – attending other people's meetings, scrolling though social media, going through the motions of doing things because you feel you must or to please others. This is time you will never get back and it is not bringing you joy or helping you towards your objectives.

You may not be able to move away from all unproductive time, but it is possible to use time more effectively. So, start with defining your personal, family, community, and professional priorities. Then, be clear about the difference between the activities that bring you joy, take you closer to your goals or ones that are simply run of the mill. Remember: all humans are creatures of habit and often do what is in front of us rather than being clear about priorities.

Remember we talked about behavioural styles? Those style differences can also cause us to use time differently. Those dominant styles tend to be task related and often lose sight of the people issues which may enable their goals and objectives. This style tries to control everything and may very well become overwhelmed and control very little. Just consider how this may affect your approach to diversity, equity, and inclusion?

Promoting styles tend to be more creative and start more than they can finish. They enjoy the start-up phase of projects but may leave critical projects unfinished as they chase after the shiny, new things. So, they may enthusiastically start a work-based project to encourage diversity, equity, and inclusion and then disappear before it has fully taken hold.

Analysing styles tend to be thorough and can get so caught up in details that they lose sight of their objectives. They may tend to keep asking for more additional data before making decisions and choices. This can lead to them wanting to understand everything about every aspect of diversity, equity, and inclusion rather than simply understanding how they are personally wired and developing their own criteria to achieve this.

Supporting styles tend to build great relationships, often try to please everyone, and have difficulty saying no. Their desire to avoid conflict will lead to them taking on too many projects, trying to please everyone and, in the end, pleasing no one, least of all themselves.

So, to be a more effective leader when it comes to diversity, equity, and inclusion, whatever your personal style, there are just two key levers to success, build your personal focus and awareness before others, plan and prioritise.

As you can become more focussed, frequently ask the question "will this activity lead directly towards improving diversity, equity, and inclusion awareness?" When people more aware of this question, it becomes a handy shorthand for focussing the wider team too. At the end of every day, review your activities. Did you spend any time on diversity, equity, and inclusion? Remember: we can all fall into bad habits and spend too much time on things that do not add value.

Where does prioritising and planning come in? After you have understood your own personal biases and beliefs, then get a clear idea of what you want to do and decide how to do it. Remember planning time will increase your available time.

Building trust is essential. Effective relationships must be built on mutual trust. This will only come from understanding each other's point of view and building it into your thinking. So, as a leader, be curious about your colleagues. Ask questions authentically and respond to the answers with interest. Building effective teams will allow you to achieve your objectives more quickly and easily. Stopping to look at the bigger picture, being willing to give and receive support as well as speaking up when things are not going the way you expected, will all improve diversity, equity, and inclusion. Not engaging its people is an organisation's biggest dissipator of energy.

Add to this the new knowledge you have of other people's behavioural styles. So, you now have another tool in your armoury to avoid conflict and miscommunication. By speaking in the other person's behavioural language.

Be a role model. Be genuine and encourage everyone to speak. Look beyond the usual respondees in a dialogue and choose others to work with you.

Give constructive feedback in a supportive and caring manner. If you see others displaying bias or inappropriate behaviours, do not condone it by inaction. Instead have a private conversation with them and encourage them to see another person's point of view.

Set up ground rules for meetings and personal interactions. Establish your personal guidelines to delay judgement and evaluation until the end of the session.

Have group discussions on various aspects of diversity, equity, and inclusion. Quite often people are unaware of others and the impact of their personal beliefs and bias.

Put signs and other reminders on the walls, desks etc. Help people to remember the possibilities inherent in having a diverse, equitable, and inclusive workplace.

Communicate the why. This is the key to motivating change and is something that is so simple yet so underestimated. In fact, communicate, communicate, communicate, and then communicate again. Present people with the why and give them the opportunity to voice their fears and ask lots of questions. Often bias is a result of fear of the unknown.

Finally, storytelling is your most compelling tool for engagement. It is the most powerful tool leaders possess influence, teach, and inspire. It is effective for learning as it builds connections for your listeners and between people and different ideas. Stories share the cultures, experiences and values that bring people together. When it comes to building communities or tribes, the stories that have in common are an important part of that connection. In organisations, the stories that leaders tell will motivate others in a way that a factual statement will not.

Good stories build familiarity and trust. They allow the listener to enter the story and learn though hearing about others. Stories can have many nuances, so they are a great shorthand to convey complex concepts in an easy to grasp way. Consider a company where the leader presents a diversity, equity, and inclusion policy. Alternatively, they should consider sharing a graphic story as to why diversity, equity, or inclusion was important to them. The listeners will have some new insights as to the reality of diversity, equity, and inclusion. They will have been influenced.

Many studies have been done about the types of learners there are in a room. They boil down to people who learn visually, people who learn through hearing discussions for instance and kinaesthetic learners – people who learn through experience or feeling. Storytelling captures all three and stories are easy to remember.

We hope our stories from the past will help you in your leadership journey. It needs just a few foundation stones to help you lead into a more diverse, equitable, and inclusive future. We wish you all the best.

9798823081665